FRANKLIN LISTENS

WHEN I SPEAK

Other books by
PAULA UNDERWOOD

Who Speaks for Wolf:
With Art by Frank Howell

The Walking People:
A Native American Oral History

Three Native American Learning Stories:
Who Speaks for Wolf
Many Circles, Many Paths
Winter White and Summer Gold

Three Strands in the Braid:
A Guide for Enablers of Learning

About the cover art *The Great Tree of Peace*

by John Kahionhes Fadden, Mohawk

Long before European settlers began to arrive in this country in the 1600's, the Iroquois Confederacy practiced representative democracy under the Great Law of Peace, symbolized by the Great Tree of Peace. References to the Great Tree were often heard in oratorical speeches from both colonial statesmen and the Iroquois when they met in Council to negotiate policies of importance to both. For example, a formal delegation of Iroquois honored John Hancock with the name, The Great Tree, on the floor of the Continental Congress June 11, 1776.

On September 17, 1988, the 201st anniversary of the signing of the U.S. Constitution, a Tree of Peace was planted in Constitution Gardens on the Mall in Washington, D.C. in honor of the contributions to the U.S. Constitution which came from the Iroquois Great Law of Peace. Chief Jake Swamp, Director of the Great Tree of Peace Society, conducted the traditional ceremony. Paula Underwood served on the Working Committee which played a large part in making this event a great success. The celebration was sponsored by Americans for Indian Opportunity, the Institute for Policy Studies, and The Meredith Fund.

A poster commemorating the link between the two Constitutions and featuring art by John Kahionhes Fadden was funded by The Meredith Fund (TMF) and given as a gift to participants at the ceremony. The art depicts the friendship between Oneida Chief Skenandoah and Benjamin Franklin as they sit beneath that great Iroquois symbol, the Tree of Peace. TMF gave permission for this painting to be used as cover art for this book.

John Kahionhes Fadden is a noted artist, born in 1938 into the Turtle Clan of the Mohawk Nation. He graduated from the Rochester Institute of Technology with a major in illustration and a minor in painting. He is a prolific illustrator of dozens of books and periodicals, including many covers. He has exhibited widely in Pennsylvania, New York, and Canada. He is generous with his art in support of Iroquois causes and education. His father, Ray Tehanetorens Fadden, has devoted much of his life to the collection of oral histories. Father and son established and maintain the Six Nations Indian Museum in Onchiota, N.Y.

FRANKLIN LISTENS

WHEN I SPEAK

Tellings
of the friendship between
Benjamin Franklin
and
Skenandoah, an Oneida Chief

by

Paula Underwood

A Tribe of Two Press
SAN ANSELMO, CALIFORNIA

FRANKLIN LISTENS WHEN I SPEAK
Tellings of the friendship between
Benjamin Franklin and
Skenandoah, an Oneida Chief

Cover Art: *The Great Tree of Peace*
by John Kahionhes Fadden
Reproduction Rights held by The Meredith Slobod
Crist Memorial Fund which commissioned this 1988
painting in commemoration of Iroquois contributions to the United States Constitution.

Designed and Produced by Bob Helberg

LCCN: 96-061961
ISBN: 1-879678-05-5

FIRST EDITION

A Tribe of Two Press
PO Box 216 • San Anselmo. CA • 94979
1 - 800 - 995 - 3320

Dedicated to my grandparents
Sarah Mariah Leonard and Oliver Perry Underwood
with deep gratitude
for their memory and for their wisdom

My Grandparents,
in front of their retirement home in
Los Angeles, California
about 1925

ILLUSTRATIONS AND NOTES

TABLE OF CONTENTS

Monument to Skenandoah on
Hamilton College Campus

SKENANDOAH is commemorated by this monument on the green lawn of Hamilton College in Clinton, New York — on land which the Oneida gave to Samuel Kirkland via their Treaty with the State of New York in 1788 and which Kirkland later gave to the Hamilton Oneida Academy. The inscription reads:

"This Memorial is erected by the Northern Missionary Society in token of their respect for the memory of Schenando A Chief of the Oneida Nation, Who died in the peace and hope of the Gospel, on the 11 of March 1816. Hist. Eloquent and brave, he long swayed the councils of his tribe whose confidence and devotion he eminently enjoyed. In the war which placed the Canadas under the crown of Great Britain, he was actively engaged against the French, in that of the Revolution he espoused the cause of the Colonies and ever afterwards remained a firm friend of the United States. Under the ministry of the Rev. Mr. Kirkland, he embraced the doctrines of the Gospel, and bravely exhibited their power in a long life adorned by every Christian virtue, he fell asleep in Jesus at the advanced age of one hundred years."

According to his wish, Skenandoah is buried near his dear friend, Dr. Samuel Kirkland, Missionary to the Five Nations.

SOURCE: Photograph and inscription courtesy of the Hamilton College Library in Clinton, N.Y.

Introduction: A Family Affair

Many Oral Keepings have been handed down in my family from my Grandfather's Iroquois Grandmother. Someone in each of these five generations has been painstakingly trained as an Oral Historian. Our purpose has been to protect and preserve all this Ancient Wisdom until this generation, when all was to be shared with those who would listen.

Franklin Listens When I Speak is one more such Keeping. It is an Oral Autobiography handed down from my grandfather's grandmother's grandfather. I was told that my Grandfather, Oliver Perry Underwood, learned all this from his Grandmother, Tsilikomah, on the Underwood family farm near Georgetown, Illinois. Tsilikomah learned this particular Oral Autobiography from her mother, Lame Deer, before 1810 in their Oneida community Caskaskia on the Shenango River in what are now called New Castle and Western Pennsylvania. Lame Deer, in her turn, heard this Keeping directly from her father, whose name has been handed down as Skenandoah (Oneida pronunciation) or Shenandoah (Mohawk pronunciation).

The image I have of these histories and traditions begin with swirling mists on a river and go on to tell the story of a young boy determined to learn — a young Benjamin Franklyn — and of many of the contributions Skenandoah made to Native Nations and to this new Nation.

Step by step, my father led me from one image to another through the decades of the 1700's in which they occurred, until the recording was complete. They are presented here just as I learned them: in the traditional manner of my People. In *Skenandoah's Song*, I am recounting what my father told me, just as he had heard it from his father, just as *he* heard it from his grandmother, and so on back to Skenandoah, whose voice you hear, as it is his Oral Autobiography which he asked his daughter to hand down the generations. When Tsilikomah adds her Mother's Story, you hear Lame Deer telling her stories about Skenandoah just as she remembered hearing them both from him and from others.

There was a great statesman and military leader named Skenandoah among the Oneida before, during, and after the Revolutionary War. Henry R. Schoolcraft gives him nine pages in his *History Of The Indian Tribes Of The United States.* However, my tradition tells me to very carefully relate what has been handed down to me and to be very slow to leap to any conclusions based thereon. As my father used to say, "Jumping to conclusions . . leads to contusions!"

It wasn't until I saw some of the traditions handed down from my grandfather's grandmother's grandfather retold by a descendant of this same Oneida statesman, Skenandoah, that I was reasonably convinced the one and the other are the same man. The aspects that seem similar are 'Skenandoah/Shenandoah' as a joking name, the various pronunciations, and the bringing of food to George Washington. In my tradition, you see, my responsibility is to pass on to you the information I have, so that you can reach your own conclusions. All perceptions, all interpretations are honored as part of the whole story.

My grandfather, then, became a young man hearing and absorbing all these Keepings with absolute accuracy — including *Skenandoah's Song.* Then in the early 1890s he met my grandmother, Sarah Mariah Leonard, in Des Moines, Iowa, at a Quaker Meeting. As they got to know each other, he was stunned to learn that she, too, kept an oral history which had been handed down in her family for generations — and this oral history related to some of the events in *Skenandoah's Song.*

Skenandoah and Benjamin Franklin were friends. Parts of their friendship are retold in *Skenandoah's Song* as it has been handed down through my Grandfather Underwood. This telling is echoed by *Uncle Ben* —a story told by my Grandmother Sarah Mariah Leonard, his wife, who was first cousin to Benjamin Franklin — several generations removed — through both of her parents going back along many lines to two of Benjamin Franklin's uncles — John and Eleazer Folger, brothers to Abijah Folger Franklin, Benjamin Franklin's mother. [This family relationship is detailed in Addendum I - A pp. 96-99.]

These recountings end with Grandmother Sarah's stories about her Nantucket ancestors — *Uncle Ben* and *John Howland's Story.* She was a wonderful little woman — patient, yet purposeful. I called her *Grandmo,* a grand grandmother. She always spelled Franklin in the older manner, *Franklyn,* and I have kept that tradition in my telling of these stories.

The fact that these histories matched each other at certain points, yet were told from two perspectives — Skenandoah and Franklin; Oliver Perry Underwood and Sarah Mariah Leonard — lent double weight to the value of this Family Keeping. They decided — and I agree — that they should be written down together.

As the lineal descendant of both traditions, I have done my very best to recount with absolute accuracy what has been handed down to me. Over the years, I have looked for written records and for other family traditions, seeking comparisons and demonstrations of probability. The results of this subsequent research and my tentative conclusions, including all three family trees, are found in Addendum I. I have recorded these adventures in learning as accurately as possible, so that the children's children's children may yet learn.

It is difficult to say which of these traditions I found more inspiring! Each gave me many of the gifts I treasure still.

Jeanne Lamar Slobod — my friend and editor — has given many patient and effective hours to further research. She is primarily responsible for the added information inset in frames and interspersed among the pages of the manuscript.

I am honored to carry the task of sharing these family keepings at this time and in this way. May there be learning here. And may these Tellings encourage others to keep the traditions of their own families.

Now,

Kind thoughts come,

Paula Underwood

REFERENCES: Henry R. Schoolcraft's biography of Skenandoah appears in Volume VI, pp. 509-518 of his *History of the Indian Tribes of the United States* collected and prepared under the Bureau of Indian Affairs as directed by Congress in 1847. Documentation for Caskaskia/New Castle is found in *Indian Paths of Pennsylvania* by Paul A. W. Wallace. The Letters to the Editor referred to are reproduced on p. 60 and p. 105.

FRANKLIN LISTENS WHEN I SPEAK

FRANKLIN LISTENS

WHEN I SPEAK

The river flowed swiftly by, a dark gray-green under the pale light of a sunless sky. Over the water white mist coiled and drifted — obscuring everything beyond a few paces. The mists were thick enough so that no one at all could bear witness from a distance. Here at the river's edge, you could scarcely see the beginning of the dock from its end. And the land disappeared in swirls of soft white.

Two boys sat on the farthest pilings, carefully folding their clothes on the dry wood. Just as carefully lowering themselves into the chill waters.

"Like this," one of them said, and stroked off across the water, one arm after the other, turned in a moment and stroked back.

"Now you try," he suggested.

Franklin, the Swimmer

Franklin grew up in Boston, a seaport town with rivers and ponds accessible. His own words have him saying "Living near the water, I was much in it and about it, learnt early to swim well." I have seen no reference in his writings to the young Mohawk boy in this story who helped him learn how to swim, but my tradition is very clear about this.

In his later life, he tells the following story: "I amused myself one day with flying a paper kite; and approaching the bank of a pond, which was near a mile broad, the weather being very warm, I tied the string to a stake, and the kite ascended to a very considerable height above the pond, while I was swimming. In a little time, being desirous of amusing myself with my kite, and enjoying at the same time the pleasure of swimming, I returned; and, loosing from the stake the string with the little stick which was fastened to it, I went again into the water, where I found that lying on my back and holding the stick in my hands, I was drawn along the surface of the water in a very agreeable manner. Having then engaged another boy to carry my clothes round the pond to a place which I pointed out to him on the other side, I began to cross the pond with my kite, which carried me quite over without the least fatigue, and with the greatest pleasure . . ."

SOURCE: *The Founding Fathers - Benjamin Franklin: a Biography in his own words.* Edited by Thomas Fleming. Newsweek, N.Y. The picture is the title page illustration in an 1852 book, *The Works of Benjamin Franklin*, and is used with permission of The American Philosophical Society.

And the younger boy took a few tentative strokes across the water, floundered a little, and returned.

He coughed, clearing water from nose and mouth.

"I'll try again," he wheezed at last.

And try again he did.

They were so similar, these two boys, and so different also. They were both close to nine. The younger, shorter boy had shoulder length blond hair and blue eyes. The other's raven-black hair was long and tied back with a thong. He was darker, too, with laughing brown eyes.

Two boys, alone in the water.

One learning to swim.

And learn he did. For he watched carefully when the taller boy swam and imitated his movements while still holding on to the dock. Pretty soon he could move about the water with some ease, turning this way and that.

"You no longer flap like a beached fish," the taller boy laughed. "You do better."

After awhile, the fog began to lift and — afraid they might be seen — they climbed out of the water and began to dress.

"No one here at all understands what we do," the younger boy pointed out. "Will you come again when next the fog settles?"

"I will try," the darker boy replied. And strode off up the dock — legs covered with buckskin, tying a feather in his hair.

The younger boy struggled into his breeches and shirt and started back for home. This time of year, children seldom wore shoes, even in Boston Towne — and home was not far.

"Who do you suppose these two boys were?" my father asked.

I was puzzled for a moment .. and then saw the clues — breeches, buckskin, a feather, Boston.

"One is Indian and one is not," I replied.

"One is a Colonist? Breeches and Boston say not too long after Colonists arrived."

"That's right, Honey Girl," he replied. "One boy grew up and we called him Uncle Ben."

"Benjamin Franklyn!" I answered at once, knowing well who in the family carried that name.

"That's right, too. What I understand from what my father said was that Franklyn, when just a lad, saw some Indians swimming and noticed how easily they crossed and recrossed the water, going in any direction at all they chose.

"This struck his mind as a useful skill and he asked to learn how it was done. No one else in Boston seemed to think people belonged in water. Yet the Mohawk sent a boy Franklyn's own age for him to learn from, and they became great friends for awhile."

"Why did you learn this from your father," I asked. "Wasn't Uncle Ben Grandmother's uncle?"

"Yes, that's right. But my father knew a lot about Franklyn — passed down from his grandmother's grandfather — the one they named the river after — Shenandoah, Skenandoah."

"Did he learn to swim? The boy who grew up to be Franklyn?"

"Far as I know, he did."

"TELL ME WHAT ELSE HE LEARNED," I asked.

AND MY FATHER BEGAN . .

Skenandoah's Song

There are things I learned about Franklyn
long before I met him.

He had a long history with our People.

IN THE OLD DAYS,
    we used to send people down into the small towns
        the New People had along the shores and rivers.

So as to give no offense,
    individuals went only,
        and as old as might be.
Men went usually . . and women sometimes.

They listened . .
    and they asked questions.
They listened to learn
    which ones might best benefit from the questions.

WE SAW HOW IT WAS —
    How this People spread themselves on the land —
        more coming all the time.

Nor did we think this would stop.

Surely our children —
    and the children after them —
        would live in a land
            much changed by their arrival.

WE COULD NOT STOP THEIR ARRIVAL.

WE CHOSE NOT TO TRY.

WE WELCOMED THEM AS BROTHERS —
    AGAIN AND AGAIN —
        and looked to see
            which ones among them
                might most easily learn.

IT WAS FOR THIS REASON
    that some among our older-heads
        went down into their villages.

They looked for those
    who were willing learners —
        and many of these were the very young.

IT WAS NOT OUR PURPOSE
    to change their ways —
        only to invite them to consider certain things.

IT WAS OUR THOUGHT THAT —
    if they are asking themselves the right questions —
        perhaps the children's children's children
            can better live with the answers.

AND SO
    we asked this one and that . .
        what occurred to them about many things . .
        and waited patiently for the answer.

THE NAMES OF MANY PEOPLE SO IDENTIFIED
    have been lost to us.

Some we still remember.
    Samuel Adams was one — as was Abigail.

An old woman used to go down
    and sit in her back garden from time to time
        where she played as a child.
           Tell a story.
           Ask a question.

When the young have a quick mind —
    you need only ask once.

The question will live with them
    for a long time . .   a long time.

PERHAPS THE BEST OF THESE —
   the only one I knew really well —
     was Franklyn.
When he moved closer to me,
   a Brother of mine came
     and asked me to watch this one - -
      to visit him when I could
        and to talk with him about the ways of men.

"He has an agile mind," my Brother said.
   "We expect much of him."

AND
   He told me how this one — Franklyn —
     had been understood from his earliest days
      as of exceptional ability.

WE SAW
   How his mind grasped quickly any new thought.

   Neither did he resist understanding
     merely because what he learned
      argued with what he thought before.

   Rather,
     he sought to include both
      in a broader perception . .
     and he kept his close counsel —
      even when young —
        in a community less given to broad thinking.

   Clearly,
     he was an exceptional person.

But all this
    I learned from another.

WHAT I LEARNED FOR MYSELF
    WAS THE REALITY OF A COMPLEX MIND

One that held a great many things
    in present focus.

For he held the thoughts and ideas before him
    all at once —
        as if wondering
            which of the many possibilities to select —
            which to add for the stew.

Then, having chosen,
    he would tuck the others away for the future —
        as if storing them in his coat pocket.

"These are not useful today"
    — he would sometimes say —
    "but who knows what tomorrow might bring."

AND
    He listened to people
        as carefully as he spoke . .
    His casual air when speaking
        belied the thoughtfulness of his words
            and when listening,
                changed to absolute concentration.

Unless, of course, it was his wish
    to convey that what was being said
        was of trivial import.
Then his eyes sought any place at all
    and hands moved now and again through air
        as if seeking something of greater substance . .
            or flicking away something exceedingly light.

He was a master at this.

His movement, this dance,
    was a devastating comment
        on someone else's lack of thought . .
    and his apparent thoughts on this
        quickly filled the room . .
    so that someone else — never he —
        was likely to challenge the speaker.

Over the years —
    I have seen him do this again and again.
        He has found it a useful device with many.

BUT WITH ME . .

FRANKLYN LISTENS
    WHEN I SPEAK —

AND
    I HONOR HIM FOR THIS.

I have met Franklyn many times,
    spoken with him often.

Sometimes taking with me someone
    whose English was better than mine.
Sometimes not.
And sometimes
    he brought with him a particular friend
        whose command of some of our languages
            was very good indeed.

But sometimes we talked alone.

And our understanding was such
    that this was possible.

I REMEMBER
    Meeting in a meadow —
        with his particular friend
            and one also he called nephew —
    This last lived not far from our community
        and became a particular friend to me also.

Franklyn joked much on this,
    as he was also a Friend,
        one of our Little Gray Brothers.

Washington Begins French & Indian Conflict at Fort Necessity

Col. George Washington at age 22 was sent by the Virginia Colony in 1754 to build a fort in southwestern Pennsylvania to protect English settlements. (See map, Addendum V, p. 114). Washington conferred with the Mingo (the name given to the Iroquois in Ohio) chiefs of that area and decided to strike against a French encampment in the area. This initial engagement was successful, marking the formal beginning of the continuing struggle between the French and the British which we call the French & Indian War.

This illustration from a 19th century book shows Washington on the attack, backed up by his Indian guides. Washington then returned with his men to Fort Necessity, to wait for reinforcements which did not come, resulting in an humiliating defeat by the French. The following year, 1755, Washington was attached as an aide-de-camp to General Edward Braddock sent to direct the English effort against the French. Knowing of the problems of provisioning in the western Pennsylvania frontier, Benjamin Franklin, according to this Oral Autobiography, went to his friend, Skenandoah, asking him to take some of his people and go with Washington to help him.

ONCE,
When I met him there,
he had a particular request for me.

A young man of his acquaintance
had a particularly difficult task —
to walk out against the French —
and having failed before,
in part for lack of food,
he had a particular desire
for some of our people to accompany them —
providing at least food from the forest.

AND SO IT WAS
That I agreed to go —
leading many of our People out
to meet this young man,
whose name was Washington.

AND SO
I came to understand
how purposeful the as-yet-young can be.

For this young man was determined to win —
where before nothing but failure greeted him.

AND THESE WERE HIS CONCERNS . .

His earlier failure gave him little repute
with the one sent from over the waters
to lead this march of men —
and so This One was deaf to any learning
This Purposeful Young Man might offer.

HE DID NOT SEE . .
he was not home in his land across the waters.

HE DID NOT SEE . .
   how the forest around him
      disallowed his usual way of war.

HE DID NOT SEE . .
   he had much to learn about where he was
      and the nature of those around him.

AND SO . .
   Rather than learn to understand
    where he was and who we were —

He sought to make the world in his own image,
   surround himself only with his own men,
     seek battle only in some chosen place
      which seemed to him familiar.

He closed his ears to all entreaty.

AND SO
   we called him Never Listens . .
    and thought little of his way.

If you have never seen such a forest
   as surrounded us then —
Let me describe it to you now —
   for well I know
     some places are flat with grass only.

THIS WAS NOT SUCH A PLACE.

RATHER,
This forest was one of many great trees —
so great . .
a man might easily disappear from sight —

so close . .
that a mere half step sideways
from any place at all
caused that disappearance.

In such a place,
any flight of arrows
was useless against the wary.

Spears could hardly be turned
from one direction to another.
War clubs only
were our weapons in such a place.

For the length of a man's arm
nearly encompassed the length of his vision
in this great forest.

It was in such a forest
that Never Listens meant to use guns
which shot bullets over a long distance.

AND SO
He sought some clearing for a battle field
in a place that held few clearings at all.
He sought open air
through which his bullets might be fired.

HE FOUND NONE.

Death of Braddock

General Edward Braddock came to the French & Indian War in 1755 full of confidence in his own abilities, having just led an impressive victory for the British in Europe.

He was contemptuous of the "colonials" and their "savage" allies and refused to listen when they tried to warn him about the nature of warfare dictated by the heavily forested terrain. "Never Listens," as he was called by Skenandoah and his people, insisted on fighting a European battle designed for open fields which led to disaster in a dense forest. Much of the enemy he faced consisted of Indians fighting on the side of the French who were able to move easily over the difficult terrain. Braddock was ambushed, wounded in battle, and died several days later — a disastrous defeat. George Washington, on the other hand, who "had two horses killed under him and his clothing torn by four balls, was not even scratched."

SOURCE: *North American Indian Wars* by Richard H. Dillon. Facts on File, N.Y., 1983. Picture from a 19th Century book.

NOW
    The Purposeful Young Man returned to his tent
        after each encounter with the one chosen to lead
           more discouraged than the day before.

AND WE TOLD HIM,

    "NEVER MIND!
        We will see you and your men are fed.
        We will protect you —
           and more from the foolishness of these English
           than from the purpose of the French."

AND SO IT WAS.
    Our People regularly brought Deer and Squirrel,
        roots and berries,

    UNTIL AT LAST
        our ways in living together brought offense
           to those around He Who Never Listens —
           and he ordered our People away.

    Many went . .
        offended at the offense.
    But some stayed . .
        enough to assure at least the survival
           of our Pale Brothers —
           if not, perhaps, for these English.

AND SO IT WAS
    THAT ONE DAY A GREAT BATTLE AROSE.

    It was poorly chosen
        and not carefully predicted.

"It would seem"
   — we said to one another —
"That Never Listens is so used to command . .
      that he thinks
         the forest will march off at his behest
      so that he can use his weapons in his usual way."

And we laughed
   at the image of a marching forest.

WE DID MORE THAN THIS.

   We warned the Purposeful Young Man
      again and again
         of the nature of this warfare . .
      and there was great danger for him —
         many bullets flying.

   WE SANG SONGS
      FOR HIS SURVIVAL —
         AND FOR THOSE HE LED.

   In our mind
      we saw him walking back toward us
         after the battle.

   WE KNEW IT TO BE SO.

AND IT WAS SO —

FOR
    HE RETURNED TO US,
        CLOTHES PIERCED THROUGH WITH BULLETS,
            YET UNSCATHED,

    AND THANKED US
        FOR OUR PRAYERS
            AND FOR OUR WARNINGS . .

    "FOR SURELY,
        BOTH HAVE HAD SOME EFFECT
        IN MY SURVIVAL."

AND THAT DAY
    Never Listens died a death of his own design,
        heedless of the warnings of others.

    "He thought he was home"
        — someone said —
            "And now . . at last . . it is so."

SO THAT IS MY TELLING
of the Purposeful Young Man.

We knew him
to be someone of consequence.

We saw for him
a broad path on the land.

WE WERE GLAD OF HIS SURVIVAL.

FRANKLYN HIMSELF
I knew for a long time.

I have been a number of times
in his shop of marks-on-pages.

He spent much time
looking for ideas to place on paper —
and found these wherever he may.

SOMETIMES
he would ask our understanding of this and that . .
and formed it into some words of his own.

He told me
much of what he wrote came from this.

FOR INSTANCE,
    there was a saying among us . .

    GREAT WIND,
      MUCH THIRD WOOD . .

I explained this to him,
    saying . .

FIRST WOOD
    is that which is lying on the ground.

    If it is recently fallen,
      it may be dry and good for any fire.

    If it has been on the ground long, however,
      it may be damp, even partly decayed.

    SO THAT
      if something comes easily to hand,
        yet may or may not have value —
    we ask
      if it is FIRST WOOD.

SECOND WOOD
    is still on trees.

    These are dry branches
      which have not yet fallen.
    These must be broken off to add to the fire.

SO THAT
   we say of anything
      which requires some effort,
         yet has clear value . .
      perhaps it is SECOND WOOD.

NOW,
   things being what they are,
      around any Community
   FIRST WOOD disappears quickly
      and SECOND WOOD soon after.

 SO THAT
   the walk for new wood
      is farther and farther.

      OR UP.

FOR
   these dead branches
      which may be higher in the trees,
         requiring some climbing,
      or at some distance,
         requiring walk-and-carry,
   this we call THIRD WOOD.

AND THIRD WOOD is the best of all . .
   yet not without risk —

As hand or foot may miss its purchase . .
  or foothold crack and fall away
    causing a sudden arrival on the Earth below . .
And distance
  may be too far from community
    to allow of real protection
      from wind or misadventure,
        allowing difficulties of its own.

SO THAT we say of anything
  which has great value,
    yet comes with no small risk —
      clearly —
        here is THIRD WOOD.

AND SO
  should a Great Storm come,
    even one which threatens the roof,

    AT LEAST,
      much THIRD WOOD
        will be gathered for us from the trees.

THUS,
  it is said among us

  GREAT WIND,
    MUCH THIRD WOOD.

Franklin's Almanack

The incident of Franklin taking an Iroquois proverb and turning it into a "morsel of Wisdom" is related in these pages. But my tradition does not say that Franklin published any of these proverbs in *Poor Richard's Almanack*. In fact, my tradition does not mention the Almanack, it simply says these sayings were translated into English by Franklin.

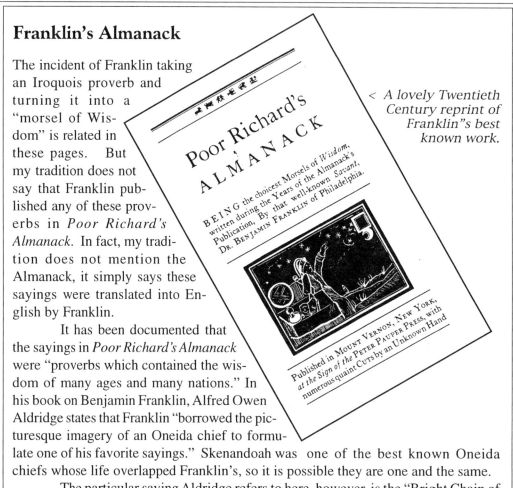

< A lovely Twentieth Century reprint of Franklin"s best known work.

It has been documented that the sayings in *Poor Richard's Almanack* were "proverbs which contained the wisdom of many ages and many nations." In his book on Benjamin Franklin, Alfred Owen Aldridge states that Franklin "borrowed the picturesque imagery of an Oneida chief to formulate one of his favorite sayings." Skenandoah was one of the best known Oneida chiefs whose life overlapped Franklin's, so it is possible they are one and the same.

The particular saying Aldridge refers to here, however, is the "Bright Chain of Friendship." This refers to the Covenant Chain and the necessity for keeping it bright which frequently turns up in Indian Council oratory on the part of both the Indians and the colonials as they exhort one another to maintain their mutual friendship and to uphold the treaty promises made on both sides.

I did not find "It is an ill wind that blows no good" in *Poor Richard's Almanack*. My reference librarian attributes it to John Heywood (1497-1575, a playwright and musician in Henry VIII's court) and phrased as "It's an ill wind that blows no man good." I have other examples of Iroquois proverbs with Franklin translations. The one related in these pages is the one that is clearest in my memory, and I have written it down exactly as I heard it. I think the story is accurate as reported. Perhaps Franklin already knew about Heywood's phrase and suggested it as the interpretation.

NOW
    Franklyn struggled to say this
        in a way which held the meaning
            in fewer words than mine.

FINALLY,
    he was decided.

    "Though it be incomplete"
        — he offered —

    "THIS I WILL SAY —

        IT IS AN ILL WIND
        THAT BLOWS NO GOOD,"

AND
    As this was explained to me,
        I saw how much, but not all,
            of the meaning was conveyed . .
                and thought myself his earlier words —

    "EVERY STORM BRINGS SOME BENEFIT"
    were clearer.

AND YET,
    He was not speaking to our People, but to his own.

AND WE CAN SEE
    by how many still listen
        that his are the words
    that are likely to be most easily remembered.

FRANKLYN'S CONCERN
for the nature of his government was great.

IT WAS THIS ABOVE ALL
THAT CONCERNED HIM.

TIME AND AGAIN
He tried to show his People
the wisdom of our way.

He printed these things in his print shop . .
and if one thought wouldn't take hold,
he would try another.

FROM TIME TO TIME
We discussed these things . .
how to engender understanding.

In this interaction,
perhaps a new way was formed . .

A NEW WAY
through which
those who have not learned
over countless generations

RESPECT FOR VARYING VIEWS
AND THE GENERAL AGREEMENT
WHICH CAN GROW OUT OF THAT RESPECT

may begin to learn
the nature of such respect.

FROM TIME TO TIME
  FRANKLYN SOUGHT OUR COUNSEL.

FROM TIME TO TIME
  WE SOUGHT HIS.

SO IT WAS AT THE TIME
  That they began to form their Union,

  AT THE TIME
    they declared themselves
      separate from their English brothers,

    EVEN AT THAT TIME
      did we join him.

      Three from the Mohawk
        came down . .

      And two from the Oneida,
        one Turtle,
        one Wolf.

      AND I WAS THAT WOLF.

June 11, 1776 — The present being provided for the Indians, they were called in, and the speech [prepared by the Standing Committee for Indian Affairs and considered by the Congress on June 6] agreed to, was delivered as follows:

BROTHERS,

We hope the friendship that is between us and you will be firm, and continue as long as the sun shall shine, and the waters run; that we and you may be as one people, and have but one heart, and be kind to one another like brethren.

BROTHERS,

The king of Great Britain, hearkening to the evil counsel of some of his foolish young men, is angry with us, because we will not let him take away from us our land, and all that we have, and give it to them, and because we will not do every thing that he bids us; [the original report includes the following sentence: "he hath taken up the hatchet to strike us, and given money to a people who are strangers to us, to come from a far country, and fight against us."] and hath hindered his people from bringing goods to us; but, we have made provision for getting such a quantity of them, that we hope we shall be able to supply your wants as formerly.

BROTHERS,

We shall order all our warriors and young men not to hurt you or any of your kindred, and we hope you will not suffer any of your young men to join with our enemies, or to do any wrong to us, that nothing may happen to make any quarrel between us.

BROTHERS,

We desire you to accept a few necessaries, which we present you with, as tokens of our good will towards you.

The presents being delivered, the Iroquois begged leave to give a name to the president [John Hancock]; the same being granted, the Onondago chief gave the president the name of Karanduawn, or the Great Tree, by which name he informed him the president will be known among the Six nations.

NOTES: This page (430) is taken from the printed version of the Journal by the Government Printing Office, 1906, edited from the original records in the Library of Congress by the Manuscript Division. The address by the Congress is recorded in the writing of George Wythe in the *Papers of the Continental Congress*, No. 30, folio 351. The Indians present for this formal occasion included other Iroquois as well as Skenandoah's small group which came to consult with Franklin. The information in brackets is added for clarification.

The name bestowed on Hancock represented a great honor as the Great Tree is the symbol of the Iroquois Confederacy. (See ADDENDUM VI, p. 115, for an explanation of the symbology.) This, and other references, clearly document Iroquois presence. This record does not say who delivered the speech to the Indians, but it illustrates the Colonial custom of adopting the Indian style of oratory when negotiating with the various Indian Nations.

OUR PURPOSE THERE
was some representation at their Council.

AND YET
THAT REPRESENTATION
WAS DENIED.

We were disallowed
from hearing their discussion
and so we limited ourselves
to a formal presentation.

These five came early
and stayed late.

WE COUNSELED MUCH WITH FRANKLYN . .
Often late at night
lit by a solitary candle.

FOR
we were not the only group
who sought and were sought by Franklyn.

Many from among them
debated long after the Council was recessed . .
arguing this and that approach.

AND
only after these were gone —
Jefferson and Adams
chief among those we knew —

only after that
did we have access to his study . .
discussing once again the manner of men
and the possibilities of understanding.

FROM ALL THIS
  I REMEMBER PARTICULARLY
    THREE THINGS . .

THE FIRST
  was the manner of our listening.

  FOR
    Franklyn was desirous
      of spending less of his evening hours
        explaining to us the nature of events.

  AND SO
    he protested loud and often
      of heat within the chamber . .
        asking some open window
          in respect of his great age.

  AND BENEATH THAT OPEN WINDOW
    in some casual way,
      two or three of our delegation came to sit,
        much as if asleep, ears always awake.

  AND, when this was allowed,
    Franklyn's evenings
      were less consumed with explanations
    and his days
      less filled with dozing . .

  FOR
    that sleep he lost in planning tomorrow's work
      he regained during lengthy debates
        he had no need to hear.

FOR,

    as he spoke often and much with us
      so had he other listening ears
        among the recognized delegations . .
    and these he had carefully instructed
      in what to do and when to wake him.

    It was his continuing nature
      to think his way down many possible paths,
        predicting probable outcomes,
      and to design responses
      which would redirect the flow of thought.

SO,

  as he dozed,
    those who were his listening ears
      remained alert,
        well prepared for possible events,
        well agreed on the nature of their response.

AND WE SAW HOW IT WAS
  Franklyn well deserved his sleep —
    and wisely left most work to men of lesser skills.

AS LONG AS THE WINDOWS OPENED
  FROM TIME TO TIME —
    JUST SO LONG
      DID OUR SMALL DELEGATION REMAIN.

ONE DAY,
    during a debate that was of particular import,
        it began to rain.

    Great pouring drops rained down,
        till all was drenched below.

OUR LISTENING EARS
    Remained where they were
        until the window closed —
    Then they asked access to the central hall
        next to the chamber for debate —
            thinking perhaps to hear through an open door
            what they could no longer hear
                through any open window at all.

FRANKLYN, HIMSELF,
    had come to the window to close it —
        indicating access through the open door
            to the central hall beyond.

    Those who guarded that door
        had no wish to allow our approach —
        and so Franklyn was sent for —

    "Can you not allow these poor Indians
        to sit here 'til the rains cease?"
            — he asked the guards.

AND
    For some time
        it was allowed . .

THEN FINALLY
    The strong smell of wet deerskin
        penetrated to the back of the Council Chamber
            through the open door.

    AND THEN
        other delegates insisted
            that the door be closed
            or that we leave,
                as they found our odor offensive.

INDEED,
    IT WAS OUR LAST OFFENSE.

The three Mohawk left for their own places,
        saying there was little else
            that they could do
                when disallowed to listen . .
            and that most seemed resolved
                that was our greatest concern.

AND YET,
    My Turtle Brother and I remained . .
        for there was still one issue unresolved
            which concerned us greatly.

    FOR
        THE FULL NATURE OF THIS NEW NATION
        WOULD BE OUR CONTINUING GIFT
            TO THE CHILDREN'S CHILDREN'S CHILDREN.

NOW
    THE SECOND THING THAT I RECALL
        WAS A DAY
            WHICH PLEASED FRANKLYN GREATLY.

    It was a day
        when all things turned from one thing to another
            on a mere phrase.

FOR
    writings went regularly back and forth
        between the woman Adams
            and the hands of her husband.

    Perhaps many of these were captured —
        one at least —
    And much was made by the captor
        of the poor thoughts
            this Adams named John
                often had of others.

    "It was a critical point"
        — Franklyn said —

    "ONE WHICH MIGHT BREAK OR MAKE
        A NEW NATION."

"When asked if I were not shocked
    by the contents of the letter read aloud,
        I saw how it was
            he asked me to take sides against Adams.

"And I wondered at his foolishness,
    giving me the whip hand like that.

"But I saw how it was
    he already thought he had won.

"And I answered him —
    expressing how greatly I was shocked —
        shocked to learn
    that anyone at all
        would presume to pry
            into the private correspondence
            of a man with his wife . .

"FOR SURELY,
    NO GENTLEMAN WOULD.

"AND ALL WAS CHANGED IN AN INSTANT.

    "What was presumed lost
        was easily gained
            by a neat turn of phrase.

    "For want of some better discretion
        on the part of its opponents
            A NEW NATION WAS BORN."

AND
    I SAW HOW IT WAS SO
    AND HAD SOME HOPE
        FOR THIS NEW NATION —
        SEEING THE WISDOM
            OF SOME OF ITS DESIGNERS.

NOW
much had passed

YET
ONE ISSUE
REMAINED UNRESOLVED.

Would this new Nation
be a Nation of free men and captive women —
or would it be a Nation of captive men as well?

AND
it was this issue
on which they now began debate.

No resolution was devised . .
and the delegates lost patience in the heat.

UNTIL AT LAST
one night
Franklyn said to me . .

"I fear we must concede, my Brother.

"Not any wisdom
I can devise
has moved them at all.

"I fear the choice
lies between a new Nation
of some men free —
or no Nation at all
nor any increase in freedom either."

AND
　　I saw his determination
　　　　and I pled with him thus . .

"I fear, my Brother,
　　you choose now a path
　　　　which leads to a war
　　　　　　greater than the one you now address —

"One
　　which a hundred years from now —
　　　　will place Brother against Brother
　　　　　　to resolve the same issue
　　　　　　　　which you now debate.

"One
　　which will exceed any war yet known
　　　　in both bitterness and blood."

"I fear me it is so"
　　— he answered —

"Yet we are not gods —
　　and cannot resolve every issue.

"Even at such cost,
　　we must move forward.

"THIS NATION
　　MUST NOT BE STILLBORN ON ANY ONE ACCOUNT —
　　　　HOWEVER VITAL IT MAY BE.

"SOME OF THESE NEEDFUL CHANGES
　　WE MUST LEAVE TO THE WISDOM
　　　　OF FUTURE GENERATIONS."

NO WORD FROM ME
WOULD DISSUADE HIM.

AND
WHEN AGREEMENT
WAS FINALLY REACHED IN COUNCIL

I RETURNED HOME AT LAST . .
AND LAID MY SORROW
ON THE EARTH.

WHEN
This sorrow was spent,
it seemed to me
I had done all I could manage
for this new Nation . .

OUR GIFT
OF BOTH WISDOM AND FOOLISHNESS
TO THE CHILDREN'S CHILDREN.

Speaking always
for the wisdom of supporting this New Way —
at least for our own People —
I moved North —
dedicating all future effort
to the well-being of our own People —

AND
NEVER SAW FRANKLYN AGAIN.

Tsilikomah's Home in Pennsylvania

NOTE: My oral traditions say that as the century turned into 1800, Tsilikomah was living in western Pennsylvania in a community I learned to call Caskaskia. On this map it is spelled Kuskusky and is located in what is now called New Castle on the Shenango River somewhat before it flows into Beaver River.

Tsilikomah learned the stories about her grandfather, Skenandoah, as told in these pages, from her mother, Lame Deer there in Caskaskia. Tsilikomah tells these stories as Lame Deer's New Voice in keeping with the manner of my People.

Tsilikomah left Caskaskia around 1810 to settle with her Quaker husband in Vermilion County, Illinois. There, she and Drucilla Underwood adopted each other as sisters, and later she adopted Oliver Perry Underwood as her grandson and began the long process of training my grandfather to be the next Keeper of the Old Things, including the stories of Skenandoah. (See Addendum 1 - B, p. 100.)

SOURCE: *Indian Paths Of Pennsylvania* (Kuskusky Paths #45-49, Map on p. 80) by Paul A. W. Wallace. Pennsylvania Historical and Museum Commission, 1993. Map used with their permission.

And Tsilikomah added
her Mother's story
to her Grandfather's Song

Franklyn was much away
   during all this time —
      so that years might pass
         between one meeting and another —
   and yet
      they persevered in understanding.

As did Franklyn
   so did my father
      work to identify that point in time
         when a small pebble might change the course
         of a mighty river.

   Yet
      the strength of this river was such
         that in some ways
            not even a boulder would suffice.

My father told me once
   that his words to Franklyn were not idle.

He had a strong vision
    on crossing a river one day
     of a mighty war
        engaging all and subsequent colonies.

"Brother against Brother"
   — was what he saw,
     and —

"Much blood in the moving waters."
   — and —

"MEN SHALL BE FREE!"
   — the words he heard —

SO THAT
   After this Strong Vision
    and Franklyn's failure
     to free all men in the new Nation —
   my father left our home
    in what I have learned to call Pennsylvania —
     never to return . .
  and made his final home among our People
   in what I have learned to call New York.

I NEVER SAW HIM AGAIN.

ANOTHER THING I REMEMBER

This was not told me by my father —
   but rather
      by someone who remembered . .

After he returned from Philadelphia . .
After it was decided
   this Nation would be half slave, half free —
     he rolled himself in his robe
     and he wept —

This man
   who was strong in battle.

This man
   who led many along difficult paths.

This man
   who toiled unceasingly
     that our Nations might support
      the new America.

This man
   who never wept.

This man
   wept for three days —
   poured out bitter tears for a bitter war —
     which he did not . .
      and yet, I *did* . . live to see.

THIS MAN . .

Skenandoah or Shenandoah?

It was good to learn that others held pieces to the puzzle of Shenandoah / Skenandoah — his joking name, the many pronunciations thereof, and that he took corn to George Washington. The Skenandoah of this oral tradition was asked by Franklin to go to western Pennsylvania to furnish food for Washington and his men during Braddock's campaign, another example of Skenandoah's support for this country.

'Skenandoah' Pride

The article on the Shenandoah National Park [Travel, June 15] was interesting and informative. I was concerned, however, by the reference to the name "Shenandoah" as "an Indian name of obscure origins."

Shenandoah is a corruption of the name of the Oneida chief "Skenandoah," whose descendants spell their name Shenandoah, or Skenandore, or other variations, to show different families. My mother's maiden name is Sarah Skenandore, my great uncle's descendants use Shenandoah, and one other line uses Schenandoah. The head chief of the Iroquois Confederacy (Six Nations of New York) is Leon Shenandoah.

The word is Oneida and translates, according to my great aunt, to "like the deer." Chief Skenandoah, when a young man, fell in love with a clan sister (a close relative), and they were forced to meet clandestinely away from the village "like the deer."

Chief Skenandoah became known outside of his own people because of his friendship with the Rev. Samuel Kirkland and because he took corn to George Washington's hungry troops when the American colonists would not help their own liberators. He was a war chief and signed several of the early treaties of peace and friendship with the new United States on behalf of the Oneida Nation of New York, one of the constituent tribes of the Iroquois Confederacy. According to the "Handbook of American Indians," the writer-ethnologist Lewis H. Morgan sometimes wrote under the pen name Skenandoah.

—*Mitchell L. Bush Jr.*

Mitchell Bush, Jr., President of the American Indian Society in Washington D.C., with other A.I.S.- D.C. members worked hard on the celebratory planting of a Great Tree of Peace on the Smithsonian Mall during the Bicentennial of the U.S. Constitution which our cover art commemorates. This "Letter to the Editor" of The Washington Post was the first of a series of three in June/July of 1986. See Addendum II on p. 105 for the two subsequent Letters.

AND
    This Tsilikoma said also . .

    You will know him by his name.

    For they named a river after him —
        the one called Shenandoah — or Skenandoah —
        or many other variations . .

    BUT THIS
        is the nature of that naming . .

MUCH BEFORE
    The War of Revolution,
        at a time
            when there was growing difficulty
                between English and French . .

    It was our thought
        that some contact
            with our gentle Brothers to the South —
                those now called Cherokee —
                was appropriate.

AND SO
　　He was chosen — my father —
　　　　to walk South
　　　　　　and find those brothers.

　　AFTER AWHILE
　　　　he came to a long and beautiful valley.

　　　　Running from North to South
　　　　　　with a broad stream down its center,
　　　　　　　　it seemed to him the best way South.

FOLLOWING THAT TRAIL,
　　He came one day to a group of hunters —
　　　　men more familiar with this place.

　　At first,
　　　　he startled them.

　　But after awhile
　　　　they accepted with some caution
　　　　　　the peaceful nature of his intent.

　　They signed to him
　　　　that this valley led many days South
　　　　　　along an easy walk . .

　　And before they parted,
　　　　he asked with his hands
　　　　　　what they called this place . .

　　"SHENANDOAH"
　　　　— they replied —

WHEREON
   my father began to laugh
     and laugh so increasingly
      that he fell on the ground,
       rolling back and forth in merriment . .

Finally, he arose . .
   tears dripping from his laughing eyes
     and explained in sign and voice . .

   "How kind of you
     to make me feel so welcome.
   "I hear you have named this valley
     after me —
      for many call me
       SKENANDOAH —
     and some
       SHENANDOAH.

   "AND NOW I LEARN
     both the river and the valley
     bear this name."

AND
   He continued South —
     full of merriment —
      and never forgot
       the valley named for him.

"Cloud Ocean"

NOTE: Those of us who have driven the beautiful "Skyline Drive" high above the Shenandoah Valley and down into the Great Smokies have probably encountered the "Cloud Ocean" referred to in these pages. Whether in or above or below the clouds, it is a wonderful phenomenon to see. Skenandoah would have made his pilgrimage on foot, following the valley path to search out the Cherokee. His first visit was probably before the French and Indian War with one or more trips taking place later on.

I particularly thank Judy Huber of Kingston, New Hampshire, for illustrating Skenandoah's "Cloud Ocean" so beautifully. Judy is a freelance artist specializing in watercolor, pen & ink, and colored pencil. She spreads her love for art by teaching drawing to children and adults as a form of creative relaxation. A major focus of her work concerns environmental issues and endangered species.

NOW
   I HAVE ANOTHER THING TO TELL . .

FOR
   When he found those Southern People,
      he spoke with them much.

He spoke . .
   about wars to come
      and the nature of peace . .
   the possibility of a new confederacy of Nations
      now called colonies,
   the nature of French and English
      and those changed in their nature
         by growing and learning here
            to be neither French nor English
            BUT COLONISTS.

One from among this Southern People
   became his great friend.

AND SO ONE DAY
   He dared to ask a question
      that had hovered in his mind . .

      "Tell me, my Brother"
         — he asked —

"It is my understanding
    that your People and mine
        lived together once . .
    and that when we divided —
        one going mainly North
        and one mainly South —
    your People said . .
        'We go to find the Southern Ocean.'

"I ask you now, my Brother. .
    where is this Southern Ocean?"

NOW
    I should tell you
        that my father had found the Cherokee
            living in the mountains —
                far from any known salt water —

They looked out now over a cluster of mountains,
    clouds spilling slowly over their peaks,
        and his friend swept out his arm
            across this panorama
                of mountain and spilling cloud . .

    "There is our Ocean"
    — he answered —

"OUR CLOUD OCEAN."

AND
   MY FATHER SAW
      THAT IT WAS SO.

AND
   THIS MEMORY, TOO,
      HE HELD WITH GREAT RESPECT.

NOW
   MY FATHER HAD ANOTHER THING TO TELL.

YET
   IN THIS HE HAD SOME HESITATION.

FOR
   neither had he seen it
   nor did he hear it
      from anyone witness to these events.

AND
   although he knew much
      of our own memory ways,
   he knew little of the memory ways
      of this other folk.

AND YET,
   THIS WAS WHAT HE HEARD . .

There was a boy
   who was wandering like an orphan in the forest.
The how of it was not known . .
   yet he was found,
      wandering and unaware of any direction.

He was a lad of about eleven years,
   a child of Westward settlers who had lost his home.

We took him in,
   kept him among us well fed and happy
      until at last
         he asked to be treated
           as were the others his age . .
         as one of our own.

NOW
    It is known
        that much is learned in earliest years . .
        and learning late begun
           is difficult to achieve.

YET
    There was one within our community . .
        bright in many ways . .
        but as yet unable to acquire
          that capacity for vision
            which leads to expanded wisdom.

SO LET IT BE,
    We counseled one another,
        that This One shall teach our new arrival.

    In this, our teacher shall at least learn better
        what he had missed before.

AND IT WAS SO . .
    This Slow in Wisdom Learning person
        turned to the learning of another
        with more concentration
          than he had shown before on his own . .
    And one and the other began a mutual dance
        that led to great accomplishment . .
    And showed at last
        that what is impossible for one
          may yet be possible for two . .

    And both young men stood forth
        as accomplished in that Spirit Learning
        from which wisdom grows.

Thomas Jefferson Remembers

". . . So much in answer to your inquiries concerning Indians, a people with whom, in the early part of my life, I was very familiar, and acquired impressions of attachment and commiseration for them which have never been obliterated. Before the revolution, the Indians were in the habit of coming often and in great numbers to the seat of government [in Virginia], *where I was very much with them. I knew much the great Ontasseté the warrior and orator of the Cherokee; he was always the guest of my father on his journeys to and from Williamsburg. I was in his camp* [in 1762] *when he made his great farewell oration to his people the evening before his departure for England. . . . his sounding voice, distinct articulation, animated actions, and the solemn silence of his people at their several fires, filled me with awe and veneration."*

—Thomas Jefferson to John Adams
in a letter dated Monticello, June 11, 1812

SOURCE: "Jefferson's Letters." Arranged by Wilson Whitman. E.M. Hale & Co.

NOTE: Skenandoah relates traditions about the Jefferson family, including Thomas Jefferson's education and Presidency, in pp. 68 - 77. Skenandoah did not know these stories from his own experience but learned them from a Cherokee friend on his visits to their territory, so I cannot be as sure of the accuracy as I am of those stories where events involved him personally.

Although the name of Jefferson's father's Indian friend was not passed down in this oral tradition, he might very well be the great orator, Ontassetté, (also spelled Outcité and several other ways) mentioned in the quotation. Jefferson was only 19 in 1762. His father, who died when he was 14, was not alive at this time, so probably young Tom attended the farewell ceremony because of the "attachment" which began in his early years. The impression it made on him was clearly present 50 years later at the time he wrote this letter.

Historical documents also tell us that Jefferson was much interested in Indian governance and had compiled extensive data toward an Indian dictionary. Unfortunately this further direct evidence of Jefferson's Indian connections has been lost.

AND SO IT CAME TO BE . .
That the child of the settlers
returned to his own . .

AND YET
retained an absolute brotherhood
with the one with whom he had learned.

AND
This One became a leader among us
renowned for his vision.

AND
The child of the settlers grew in stature
and returned to us from time to time . .
bringing a trusted one with him
of the darkest hue . .
whom he also called Brother.

AND
He gave us to understand
that This One also might speak for him . .
So that — even could he not come —
he could send his darker Brother.

NOW
    Over time
        there was much back and forth between us . .
    So that
        what had been a good knowing
            — one of the other — continued to be so.

AND
    when a son was born to this child of the settlers,
        he asked his Brother among us
            to be as Second Father.

AND SO HE WAS,
    Consulting often on education,
    Coming to speak with the boy,
        who was growing in understanding.

AND SO IT WAS
    That one day this darker Brother
        came to us saying his master was dying . .
            for only in our world could he truly be Brother.
    And he asked his Brother among us
        to have a careful eye on his son —
        who had now fourteen years —
            and to consider the nature of his learning.

SO IT WAS
    That this Brother among us
        traveled to that other home
            at least once before any winter
        and building a shelter behind the main house . .
            would consult with this growing young man
                on the nature of learning.

NOW
   His age and temperament were such
      that this young man
         showed no eagerness to learn . .
            even from a Second Father
         thinking himself the better judge,
         seeing one way and the other often unconnected.

AND SO IT WAS
   That this Second Father devised questions,
      for which he sought answers
         among the learnings
            this young man gleaned in his studies . .
      asking if this or that way of thought
         could be found anywhere in the writings
            of this people so lately arrived.

AND SO IT WAS
   That this young man
      studied ancient peoples from beyond the waters . .
         how it was they lived one with another . .
         how it was they decided in community
         and how they assured these decisions . .

   And the young man learned well . .
      knowing as he did what questions would follow . .
      and disliking these questions less and less.

      Seeing their relevance more and more . .
         so that he increasingly
            studied the nature of affairs among men —
            the possibilities of their governance.

WINTERS CAME AND WENT.
  The meetings between these two
    less frequent.

  The last meeting of all,
    my father learned but late.

  FOR THIS LEARNING YOUNG MAN
    grown to a great height in both mind and body,
      led the thoughts of many
        who were gathered at the separation
          of these colonies from that other land,
      and led in their joining toward one Nation.

AND THE LAST MEETING
  Between this Tall Man and his Second Father
    was in this new Nation's capitol . .
      where this tall and learning man sat
        as FIRST AMONG ALL.

  "Ask me no more questions, my Father"
    — He Who Was First petitioned —

  "For my head buzzes with too many now
    and pains with my inability to answer them."

  AND
    His Second Father
      saw the pain in his eyes . .
      and saw how great a burden
        had been placed on this man
          to understand two worlds . . two ways . .
      and had no heart to increase his anguish.

AND SO
   He folded away the paper
      on which were written the thoughts of his People
      on which they asked consideration
         from this Brother to Many —
            of their Way
            and their Life
            and their Needs
         constrained
            by the closeness of these Westward settlers

   He folded the paper away
      and counseled this First Son of a Second Father
      and spoke to him thus . .

"In this Life"
   — he told him —

"More is always seen
   than is accomplished.

"You have learned our way
   better than you know . .
   Served your new Nation
      better than you realize . .

"Leave somewhat
   to the children's children.
      For surely among them
         will be some Wisdom also."

HE TURNED
   and left behind him
      this First Son of a Second Father,

LEFT HIM FOR THE LAST TIME . .
   Full of respect for a quality of learning . .
   Full of understanding of the heaviness
      such isolated understanding may bring . .
   Full of awareness of one Life well spent.

   "I thank you, my Brother,
      for this great gift of your son,"
         —he said within his heart —

   "We may both rejoice
      at great learning growing into wisdom.

   "Seeds scattered on a ready Earth
      will yet bear further fruit."

And he left
   this new capitol of a new Nation,

Never to see again the face of his Brother's Son . .
   who understood possibilities
      beyond the reach of accomplishment.

AND YET
   THEY HONORED HIS NAME
    AND THAT NAME
     WAS JEFFERSON.

Thomas Jefferson

Grandmother's Songs

My gentle little Quaker grandmother, my father's mother, sat always in her rocking chair — dressed in black, Quaker gray for Sundays, with perhaps the extravagance of a lace collar.

And always a black hat.

Small boned, light in stature — she had wondrous eyes and an inquiring mind.

She came from ancient stock, she told me.

"Some came on the Mayflower and some did not. Settled — a lot of them — on an island off the Massachusetts Coast.

"But I was born in Iowa. So was your other grandmother.

"Known each other for a long time.

"My family's kept a passel o'stories — tellings your grandfather would say — about Ben Franklyn and about that Mayflower crossing."

These are the stories my grandmother told . .

Uncle Ben

Uncle Ben we always called him. Some o' these stories, I guess, he'd let on to — but others, not at all.

One of the first things I learned about thy grandfather, (always when she told the old stories the Quaker thee's and thou's would begin) one o' the first things I learned is that he held some of the same stories.

That's what thy father wishes I share with thee now.

IT WAS LIKE THIS . .

Our Uncle Ben was a wise man — wise beyond his years from early on. Your grandfather said that was part him and part Mohawk learning. As to that, I don't know. What I do know is this.

John and Abigail Adams was the writin'est pair you ever heard of. If he didn't write her — then she was writin' him. And these letters went back and forth by fast post. You see — like a lot o' men — ol' John counted on his wife to keep him informed bout a lot o' things — not just kitchen talk either! She was a smart woman, and he knowed it.

Franklyn — he kind of thought a lot o' those letters went by slow post — Adams used to say to Abigail what he couldn't say to anyone in Philadelphia. Ben Franklyn said he afterwards suspected more than one passed through other hands on its way to Massachusetts.

You remember, child, Boston is an English name, but Massachusetts is Indian. Story o' this country I like to think! When you say Boston, Massachusetts — you've told the story of the beginnings of this nation.

Anyways, here come this big, important man — forget his name — and he brung with him this letter. And here stands John Adams, you see, and a couple o' other folk — and Ben Franklyn comes by at last.

"Let me read this to you, Dr. Franklyn," says the important man — and Uncle Ben sort o' nods — and the man begins readin' this letter from Adams to Abigail saying how it was some men there gathered were driving him to distraction — and he starts quotin' chapter an' verse on who had the least brains.

Now this was a parlous time. Ben Franklyn figured out long ago this Nation needed unity and separation from our English brothers.

"Nothing worse than a long rope," he sometimes said. "It restrains without guiding." Pretty good, I always thought.

And Franklyn also knew this was one of those times when "a few words either way proclaim the destiny of Nations." And so all the while this important man is reading all Adams' comments about men too small to hear any criticism of themselves — he's wonderin' how many letters they had to intercept to find one so negative.

And then he thought "privacy" — and then he knew what to say.

For when that important man asked him if he wasn't shocked to hear such a letter —

"Shocked," he answered, "indeed I am shocked — for who would undertake to invade the privacy of a man's communication with his wife? Surely, no gentleman would!"

And said as it was before witnesses, gathered most like by the important man to hear Ben Franklyn's answer, his twisting of one thing to another rapidly spread through all the delegations — discrediting complete the most important man against union and separation.

It made, Franklyn told us, a laughing stock out of the major opposition — made them seem so desperate to defeat us that they would stoop to any underhanded trick.

It opened the way to Union. And it taught Ben a good lesson.

"Never put on paper what you have no wish to hear read from tomorrow's pulpit," he used to say. And he lived by that. Careful about what he said, but three times careful about what he wrote.

He was like that — my grandmother went on — always making the most of everything. Exploring all the time. He never failed to learn from anyone. You remember that, child! Learn from everyone. He never cared if you were Indian or white, rich or poor, lettered or unlettered. He was in this Life to learn . . and he knew it!

He knew it so early that it cost a heep o' trouble. Don't figure he wrote this down anywhere — but when he was real young he was contracted out as an apprentice — don't matter as what. He figured out real soon that what he was doin' wasn't what he wanted to do — he went back to his pa and asked to change. "Wanted to study printin' instead," he said.

Now that might be alright except for this — the man you were apprenticed to paid your family for your help. And that pay was goin' to be a dowry for one o' Franklyn's older sisters — don't know which one.

Now she was about to marry a man she thought right much of. But that needed the dowry. And now little Ben wanted that money given back so he could learn to print.

Now it was him against her — cause if the money was given back, she didn't think her beau would wait for her family to save more — Ben was the youngest boy and no one else could be contracted for.

So he ran away. Made his own decision and ran away.

His sister was madder than any wet hen. She was right, too! Her beau didn't wait and married someone else.

She never forgave him. But he learned to print — and we're all glad he did. He tried to make it up to her, too. Took care of her and her children again and again. Helped all his folks, but this was long after he had his way — and learned to print.

Grandmother
Sarah Mariah Leonard Underwood

NOTE: My Quaker grandmother is seen here in her best Sunday dress, posing for her photograph out in the sunshine in front of their home. This probably was taken around 1928.

The picture I have in my heart is Grandmo sitting in her rocker, reading aloud either from her Bible or from Shakespeare.

My brother and I loved the rhythm of the flow of her words. We would dance and dance round the room to the sound of her voice.

She was a small woman, and I like to compare her to a bird picking up every morsel of a thought or idea, looking at it this way and that, and making a decision as to its worth. She was gentle, kind, and fair. She was also decided, firm, and determined.

(See Addendum I - A, pp. 96 - 99 for her relationship to Benjamin Franklin.)

My grandmother told me other stories, too — about how it was to be Ben Franklyn's wife — and how she could understand that, too, as her husband had been so smart and known so much.

"But you know a lot, too, Grandma!" I told her. "You know Shakespeare (I usually called him Shaky Spear) and the Bible!"

Well, your grandpa knew them, too, child — and more besides.

Our family knew Deborah well. She was younger than Franklyn . . young enough to seem more of a cousin to those of that age than Franklyn himself. So it was that they called her cousin, yet called him Uncle.

She was sad at the many partings, yet resolved to manage her affairs well in the face of the separations his greatness required.

When he begged her forgiveness for one more absence of some endurance, she answered him thus . .

"Thee has given me so great a gift," she said, "in making me thy wife . . that I can ask for little else.

"I strive in all things to learn from thee . . and to raise myself up to such a level that I may sit beside thee with some ease.

"And yet I find I cannot. For I see too clearly the greatness of thy nature . . and how the world shapes to thee.

"So I content myself with this small shop . . and with the management of household things.

"These are my busy-ness. Be you about yours."

It was like my grandmother to speak thus — changing from one way to another — so that she spoke the language of the story she told . . changing to her Indiana 'plain speech' when she told her own story.

She told me how we were related to "Uncle Ben."

"Must be on the female line," she said, "as none of us was ever named Franklyn."

And so I searched for this connection when I'd grown — traced each of his sisters — any nieces — and found no connection at all.

And yet, when I toured the White House for the first time and came round the corner — I was brought up short by the painting on the wall.

"Dad!" I said to myself. "What are you doing there?"

The face was right — the eyes and the baldness pattern — even glasses on the nose. But the hair was too long and the clothes too formal —

Just then the guide came round the corner.

"I see you staring at that painting," she began, "and, yes, it's Benjamin Franklin. That's supposed to be the only portrait he ever sat for — all the others were painted from the artist's memory."

And then I saw how it was my father looked in my own memory. Just like that portrait of Franklin — but with a shorter hair cut and an Indian nose — his Eagle beak he used to call it.

After many years and much research, I wrote a man with the name Benjamin Franklin Folger — Adelaide Folger was my grandmother's mother — and therein lay the connection.

For when he sent me a copy of his detailed genealogy, I saw that Peter Folger was Benjamin Franklyn's grandfather. His daughter had married Josiah Franklyn. His son, John Folger, settled with him on Nantucket Island.

The Folgers mainly became Quakers — and were Quakers still in my grandmother's generation — My grandmother was not Benjamin Franklyn's niece, but his first cousin six times removed — the "Uncle" a common courtesy to an older, respected cousin.

"As to the swimming," my grandmother said, "I wouldn't know."

But when I went to London, I was regaled by another tour guide, as to how that famous American — Dr. Benjamin Franklin — used to give swimming demonstrations up and down the Thames — with amazed English people hanging off the bridges and lining the shore.

Northern Europeans of that day, she said, didn't swim. They considered water cold and dangerous to health. Even sailors didn't learn the knack — preferring a quicker drowning should the ship sink.

But Indians had swum for a long time — my father said.

And a boy named Franklyn wanted to learn.

John Howland's Story

John Howland sailed across the Atlantic on the Mayflower. He is one of our most important ancestors. He signed the original Mayflower compact and was a leader in his time. This is his story, which we have told from generation to generation ever since . . to remind us of purpose and dedication.

About half-way across the Atlantic a big storm brewed up. There was thunder and lightning, waves climbing higher and higher. Everyone was hiding below deck. Not a soul was out. Even the mariners were hiding from the storm. Everything was lashed down tight.

On the third day of the storm, John Howland got sick to death of being cooped up. Couldn't even breathe much any more. So, in spite of the storm, he went up on deck to catch a breath of fresh air.

While he was standing there, a huge wave came up sudden. It covered the whole ship and just swept him right overboard!

He didn't know what to do. There he was in the middle of the Atlantic ocean with waves so high he couldn't even see the ship. He couldn't even be sure which direction to swim in, but he swam anyway. Said later that it, "just seemed straight ahead to me."

He swam until he felt that sinking was easier than swimming. One last time he gave a stroke . . and with that stroke . . he prayed.

"Oh Lord," he prayed, "If it be Thy will that my life here end, then so be it! But if Thou hast some greater purpose for my life, then let me find a way back to that ship."

And just then he took one more stroke forward . . and his hand hit a rope.

He grabbed that rope and held on for dear life! Didn't even know what the rope was attached to, but thought it had to be the ship.

He held on so long that his hands didn't seem to be part of him any more. After awhile, he wasn't sure whether he was alive or dead. He thought, "Maybe Hell is cold and wet, not burning hot!" But he held on. God had given him that rope . . and he wasn't going to let go.

After a long time . . no one has any idea how long it was . . a sailor came up on deck to check to be sure everything was still lashed down. He saw that one rope going straight out into the ocean. He thought, maybe it was a cask of water, which they could ill afford to loose. And he started hauling on the line.

To his surprise, the weight on the other end of the line turned out to be a human being. He said that our ancestor, "Came out of the ocean looking more like a drowned rat than a human being!"

But all of us from that time to this have been glad of his purpose. Purpose, you see, starts with willing sacrifice . . and goes on from there.

If you place your life in the hands of the Lord . . and accept willingly whatever it pleaseth Him to send . . it is amazing what you can survive and what you can go on to do.

This was my grandmother's story which she told me when I was very small. Many, many years later I met a very interesting woman in Washington D.C. Our extensive conversation on the possibilities of politics left me eventually explaining the attitudes inherited from my ancestors. When I told John Howland's story, she was amazed!

"You grew up with that story, too? I always heard about how John Howland fell overboard and was pulled out of the ocean!"

It turned out, you see, that we were cousins unrecognized. John Howland's story helped us recognize one another and bound us together in ways that could not have happened otherwise. Norie Huddle and I have never really been out of touch since. Our lives continue to weave together.

Memories like this — told and retold — bind families together, make our common ethics clear, help us with future decisions.

These family memories began with Benjamin Franklin learning how to swim .. and end with John Howland struggling through an ocean he had no skill in swimming.

These many Tellings handed down through my father's family help me to know who I am, who I belong to, what I need to remember.

May it be so for us all.

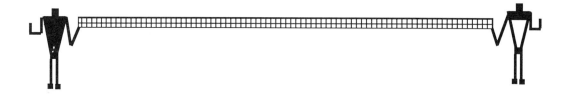

Acknowledgments

Gratitude Comes . .

First, foremost, and without exception — gratitude flows in abundance to Jeanne Lamar Slobod — friend, editor, and loyal companion through many conundrums. Her unflagging support and abettance over the years have been amazing in their effect. She is Enabler in Chief of all that's been accomplished.

Now, gratitude comes to the many members of our educational program, The Past Is Prologue Learning Way (PIP), who have read, listened, advised, and suggested revision — Cecilia Dearborn, Karen Hosey, Linda Kekina, Lisa Klein, Shari Majumder. They tell me a book like this would be a welcome source of Alternative History, an additional perspective on a critical time in American History.

To Judy Barrett and Bob Helberg — the other two legs on which A Tribe of Two Press stands — go gratitude indeed. Judy is the calm and steady pilot of our daily course and Bob is the creative designer of this book and many other ways of sharing.

Over the years many forms of assistance have come from Molly and Hu Root, who have close ties with Hamilton College in Clinton, New York. As I learned from them, Hamilton was originally the Oneida Academy under the leadership of the excellent Samuel Kirkland, a Methodist Minister and close friend to Skenandoah. Both Kirkland and Skenandoah are respectfully buried on the grounds of Hamilton College, a wonder to behold. For the Roots' hospitality, their substantial support for our educational program and the Oral Histories — gratitude truly flows! And to Hamilton College as well for their hospitality and research and for providing me with pages of Kirkland's Journals, the picture of the Monument to Skenandoah, and the Memorial Address of Elihu Root.

And gratitude flows once more to those who have fiscally enabled this volume — to The Meredith Fund, to Hu and Molly Root, and to Jeanne and Bob Slobod.

The completion of each circle of community is enabled by its many members and their common purpose. This is the Circle of Community that has enabled this present volume.

Gratitude truly comes to each and to all.

Paula Underwood

NOTE: See page 110 for an entry from Rev. Kirkland's Journal citing a visit to his friend Skenondon, giving us yet again another spelling of Skenandoah's name.
        See also p. 8 for a photo of the monument to Skenandoah on the Hamilton College campus and the inscription on the monument.

Addenda

TABLE OF CONTENTS:

ADDENDUM I. Genealogy: Introduction

The three family trees, and the accompanying notes that follow each one, detail the complex interweaving of my ancestry that led to the telling of matching family stories from several sources.

I started out on my genealogical search to find my relationship to Benjamin Franklin and to my grandfather's grandmother, Tsilikomah, who is the lineal source for the vast Oral History and other traditions we are sharing. Since written records come from a time when Indians were "invisible" (literally not counted), western style documentation proved exceedingly difficult, but not impossible. In the process, so many fascinating family details came to light that this search became a treasure trove, substantiating and weaving together many individual elements.

The Western world has a very different concept of relatedness than the Native world does. In many Native traditions, generations tend to collapse into each other. This generationally-integrated condition comes about when past and present fulfill *one responsibility* and become, therefore, the holders of *one functional unit or office continuing on.* From my perspective, it wasn't important whether Tsilikomah was Skenandoah's daughter or grand-daughter or even if she were a direct descendant. At that point in my letter to the Editor (p. 105), I called her his daughter, but due reflection reminded me that I was told there was another generation, her mother's, between them.

The Tellings of Skenandoah themselves were always clear. Fundamental accuracy is considered essential. I was always told that in the Native world, "Father to my Spirit" was/is considered more important than mere physical fatherhood. "Grandmother to my Learning" was/is considered more important than blood kinship. Long ago I accepted Tsilikomah, and the long line of Keepers of the Old Things that went before her, as Grandmother to my Learning of the Ancient Wisdom which she possessed and which she intended to be a gift for the children's children's children.

95

Folger Family Chart

Note: Folger descendants appear in bold face

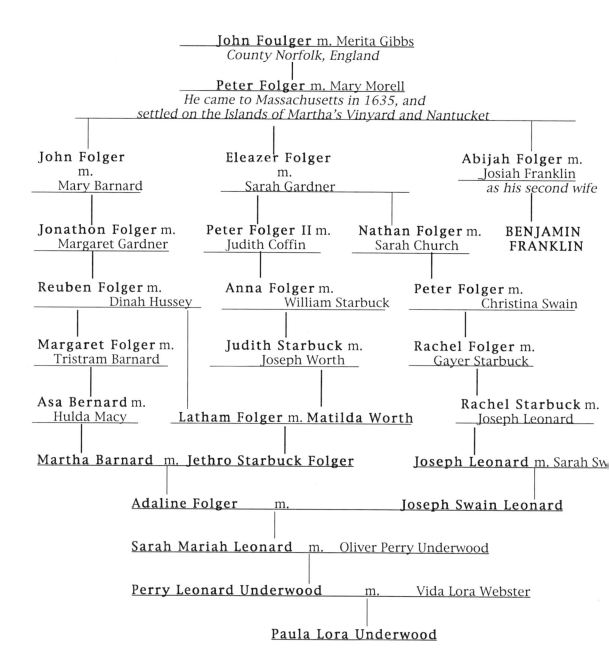

John Foulger m. Merita Gibbs
County Norfolk, England

Peter Folger m. Mary Morell
*He came to Massachusetts in 1635, and
settled on the Islands of Martha's Vinyard and Nantucket*

John Folger
m.
Mary Barnard

Eleazer Folger
m.
Sarah Gardner

Abijah Folger m.
_Josiah Franklin
as his second wife

Jonathon Folger m.
Margaret Gardner

Peter Folger II m.
Judith Coffin

Nathan Folger m.
Sarah Church

**BENJAMIN
FRANKLIN**

Reuben Folger m.
Dinah Hussey

Anna Folger m.
William Starbuck

Peter Folger m.
Christina Swain

Margaret Folger m.
Tristram Barnard

Judith Starbuck m.
Joseph Worth

Rachel Folger m.
Gayer Starbuck

Asa Bernard m.
Hulda Macy

Latham Folger m. **Matilda Worth**

Rachel Starbuck m.
Joseph Leonard

Martha Barnard m. **Jethro Starbuck Folger**

Joseph Leonard m. Sarah Sw

Adaline Folger m. **Joseph Swain Leonard**

Sarah Mariah Leonard m. Oliver Perry Underwood

Perry Leonard Underwood m. Vida Lora Webster

Paula Lora Underwood

ADDENDUM I - A. Folger Family Ancestry

As the accompanying chart shows, Sarah Mariah (Leonard) Underwood was first cousin to Benjamin Franklin on four different lines, twice each through two of Abijah/Abiah (Folger) Franklin's brothers — John and Eleazer Folger — who were of course Benjamin Franklin's uncles. Therefore, Sarah Underwood was first cousin to Benjamin Franklin 6, 5, 6, and 6 times (generations) removed, respectively. As the chart shows, both her mother and her father were Benjamin Franklin's first cousin, several times removed.

These traditions were generally known throughout the family, but came down most clearly through two Folger descendants named Starbuck — Judith Starbuck (m. Joseph Worth) and Rachel Starbuck (m. Joseph Leonard) — both of whom told these family traditions to Matilda Worth Folger (daughter of Judith) in Guilford County, North Carolina.

Judith Starbuck Worth was born in Nantucket in 1743 and would have had ample opportunity to learn the earliest traditions about Benjamin Franklin from older family members. Judith Starbuck and Gayer Starbuck, Rachel Starbuck's father, were cousins — both grandchildren of Jethro Starbuck on Nantucket.

Judith and many of her relations removed from Nantucket to North Carolina before the Revolution. We can assume the events during the Revolution were learned through letters or visits back and forth.

Rachel Starbuck Leonard was the granddaughter of Peter Folger, who was named after his famous great-grandfather, and I was told took responsibility for family traditions very seriously.

Matilda Worth Folger took these traditions with her to Indiana and told them in turn to her granddaughter, Adaline Folger, in Rush County, Indiana. Adaline told them to her daughter, my grandmother, Sarah Mariah Leonard, many times when she was a girl. She, in turn, told them directly to me.

In his *History of Nantucket,* p. 740, Alexander Starbuck says of Peter Folger the elder:

> Savage in his Genealogical Dictionary in describing Peter Folger, the first of the name to be connected with Nantucket, says that he came from Norwich, County Norfolk, England in 1635, went early from Watertown to Martha's Vineyard, probably with Thomas Mayhew. He bestowed great pains in teaching the Indians, as successor to Mayhew, and removed about 1663 to the island, where his name has ever since been in high regard.

> Nathaniel Barney says of him (unpublished ms.) "Peter Folger of whom Cotton Mather speaks 'as a pious and learned Englishman' has been named as the interpreter for Tristram Coffin Senior when he first visited Nantucket. He was the only child of John Folger, whose wife was Meribah Gibbs, and came from Norwich, England, a widower, in 1636, having his residence at some time thereafter at Martha's Vineyard. Peter married Mary Morrill in 1644, having bought her of Hugh Peters, to whom she owed service, and paid the sum of £20, which he very gallantly declared was the best appropriation of money he had ever made. Their children were two sons and seven daughters, the last of who, Abiah, was born at Nantucket in 15th of August, 1669. She was the mother of Doct'r Franklin, and her visits to her relatives here were very frequent, even in her old age."

Elsewhere I have read that Peter Folger was famous as a translator for the Indians, but would never agree to translate in the negotiation of treaties until he had assured himself that the people he was translating for would live up to their treaties. Later, he would come back to check and call anyone to task who failed to live up to the treaty.

Given these facts, Benjamin Franklin's uniqueness becomes more understandable. He had outstanding ancestry. His mother's father was more concerned with fairness than with profit, more concerned with doing right than being "right", and had a profound regard for Native Peoples.

SOURCES: Family traditions as described. Recent generations have been substantiated by certificates of birth and death, as well as probate records.

Records from The Quaker Collection, Guilford College, North Carolina.

The History of Nantucket, County, Island, and Town, by Alexander Starbuck, 1969, reprinted by C.E. Tuttle, Rutland, Vermont, 1976.

"James and Lydia (Gorham) Worth of Nantucket, Massachusetts, and Their Wandering Children", by Elizabeth Pearson White, C.G., F.A.S.G., F.N.G.S. and Edwin W. Coles, in *National Genealogical Society Quarterly,* Vol. 76, No. 4, December, 1988.

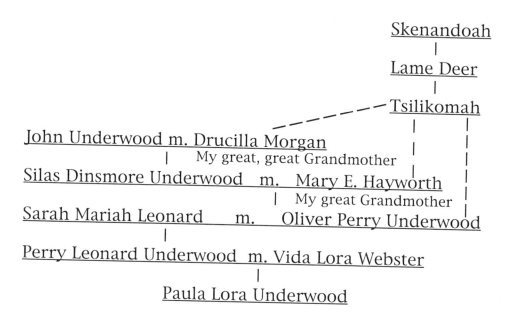

Skenandoah
|
Lame Deer
|
Tsilikomah

John Underwood m. Drucilla Morgan
| My great, great Grandmother
Silas Dinsmore Underwood m. Mary E. Hayworth
| My great Grandmother
Sarah Mariah Leonard m. Oliver Perry Underwood
|
Perry Leonard Underwood m. Vida Lora Webster
|
Paula Lora Underwood

Drucilla Morgan Underwood called Tsilikomah "my Indian sister". Tsilikomah was in Vermilion Co., Illinois when the Underwoods arrived from (West) Virginia (ca. 1825). She healed their daughter from an apparently-fatal fever. They were very close from that day on. After Tsilikomah's husband died, she lived in a cabin behind the farm house of John and Drucilla (Morgan) Underwood which John Underwood built or refurbished for her out of gratitude for his daughter's life.

Mary E. Hayworth came from a long line of Cherokee and English Quakers. As a girl, she studied the Old Things for several years with her adopted sister, Tsilikomah's only daughter. This daughter died young in child birth. At the age of 27, on 11 Dec. 1862, Mary Hayworth married Drucilla (Morgan) Underwood's son, Silas Dinsmore Underwood, as his second wife. My grandfather was their first child. According to Elmo Underwood, a cousin who was raised near Georgetown, Mary Hayworth was a prominent speaker at Quaker meetings — her husband was very proud of her and bought a span of black horses and a carriage to take her to such meetings. She transferred to the Iroquois County (Illinois) Quaker Monthly Meeting on 3 December 1870, after her last child was born. She died on 9 May 1872, when my grandfather was 9 years old. Years before, Tsilikomah had adopted Mary Hayworth as her second daughter and had been teaching her all the Old Things (Oral History, Learning Stories, and this Oral Autobiography). However, Mary Hayworth Underwood died before being able to pass on these Oral Learnings to some one of her own choosing. She thought her first son, Oliver, a likely candidate.

After his mother had died and at the age of 16, my grandfather, <u>Oliver Perry Underwood</u>, was sent by his grandmother, Drucilla Morgan Underwood, to learn from her "Indian sister", Tsilikomah. That would be ca. 1879, as he was born 27 October 1863. He then studied with her until she died ca. 1891. When he reached the age of 19, Tsilikomah formally adopted Oliver Perry Underwood as her Grandson in the manner of our People. She died about nine years later, several months after the Battle of Wounded Knee (29 December 1890), at which time she counted her age as 113, therefore born ca. 1778. As she was not Christian, as her adopted sister, Drucilla Underwood, had died in 1884, and as my grandfather was in the Dakotas researching the events at Wounded Knee for her at the time of her death, she was denied burial in the Underwood cemetery and was buried without ceremony in an unmarked grave behind her cabin near Georgetown, in Vermilion County, Illinois. I have visited this area, and it is as it was described to me.

On one of my visits, a cousin of mine in her late 70's, Sarah Young, took me on a tour of the Underwood farm, which she and her husband had once owned and farmed. When I asked her if there had ever been a cabin out in the woods behind the farmhouse, she answered, "No-o-o . . Oh, *that's right.* . . I remember it from when I was a little girl."

My grandfather Oliver Perry Underwood's wife, Sarah Mariah Leonard, descended from Peter Folger (see Folger Ancestry chart on p. 96) and was my source for the two stories, *Uncle Ben* and *John Howland's Story* included in this book.

The story of this purposeful family and their struggle to preserve an ancient wisdom begins with Tsilikomah and stretches over five generations. It will be told in detail in *A Tribe of Two,* a manuscript now (1996) under preparation.

Perry Leonard Underwood

My father was born on his parents' farm in Lone Pine Township near Lincoln, Nebraska on April 14, 1900. When he was a young man, the family moved to Long Beach, California. This photograph was taken in Huntington Park, California about 1944. I can never be grateful enough to my father for his never-ending patience with my learning!

ADDENDUM I. - C.
Howland Family Ancestry

Both John Howland and Elizabeth Tilley were on the May-flower. She was a minor child at the time in the company of her parents, John Tilley and Joan (Hurst) Rogers. John Howland came over as the indentured manservant of John Carver, who became the first governor of New Plimoth Colony in Massachusetts. John Howland was the 13th person to sign the Mayflower Compact.

Elizabeth Tilley's parents died that first difficult winter and she was taken in by the Carvers. Later they, too, died leaving John Howland their heir. John and Elizabeth married and lived into their 80s.

Governor Bradford records the final installment of John's ocean adventure thus: "It pleased God that he caught hould of ye halliards which hunge over board, and rane out at length; yet he was held up . . . and then with a boat hooke and other means got into ye ship again." [William Bradford, *History of Plimoth Plantation*, pp. 92-93, Boston 1898.]

The connection with John Howland and Elizabeth Tilley is shown on the Family Chart on the following page.

The last two generations moved from Nantucket to Guilford County, North Carolina before the Revolutionary War and on into Indiana.

As you see from the Howland chart, Judith Starbuck and Matilda Worth share Folger and Howland ancestry.

In the last generation shown on the chart, both Matilda Worth (grand-daughter of Anna Folger) and Latham Folger descend from Peter Folger. For the succeeding generations of Matilda and Latham, see the Folger Chart on p. 96 which shows the intermingling with the Leonards and the Underwoods and brings them down to the contemporary time of the author of this book.

Howland Family Chart

<u>John Howland   m.   Elizabeth Tilley</u>
John & Elizabeth's first child was:

|

<u>Desire Howland (b. Plymouth ca 1625) m. Capt. John Gorham</u>
Their 9th and last child was:

|

<u>Shubael Gorham (b. Barnstable MA 1667) m. Puella Hussey</u>
Their 3rd child was:

|

<u>Lydia Gorham (b. Barnstable MA 1701) m. Joseph Worth of</u>
Their 6th child was: <u>Nantucket</u>

                              <u>Wm Starbuck m. Anna Folger</u>
                                             |

<u>Joseph Worth (b. Nantucket 1729)   m.   Judith Starbuck</u>
Their 3rd child was:

|

<u>Mathilda Worth (b. Nantucket 1758)   m. Latham Folger</u>

SOURCES:

The Quaker Collection, Guilford College, North Carolina.

The History of Nantucket, County, Island, and Town, by Alexander Starbuck, 1969, reprinted by C.E. Tuttle, Rutland, Vermont, 1976.

John Howland of the Mayflower, Vol. 1, The First Five Generations Documented Descendants Through his first child Desire Howland and her husband Captain John Gorham, by Elizabeth Pearson White, Pictor Press, Maine, 1990.

ADDENDUM II.
Letters to the Editor of The Washington Post

NOTE: These two Letters to the Editor of *The Washington Post* in 1986 complete the series of three written in June/July 1986. (See p. 60 for the first one of the series by Mitchell L. Bush, Jr. concerning the naming of the Shenandoah River and Valley.) The third letter is my own under the name of Paula Spencer, my married name at that time.

< Rick Rio's letter to the
Washington Post, *June 28, 1986*

'Skenandoah' (Cont'd.)

Mitchell L. Bush Jr. is misinformed as to the orgins of the name "Shenandoah" [" 'Skenandoah' Pride," Free for All, June 21]. While a similar word may be part of the Iroquois language in upstate New York, the Senedo Indians of the Valley of Virginia are the accepted source of the name "Shenandoah." An early Swiss explorer, Louis Michelle, drew a map in 1707 in which Massanutten Mountain was labeled "Cenuntua." Baron de Graffenreid, in describing Michelle's discoveries, refers to a "mountain Senantoa." Other spellings have included "Chanithor," "Gerando," "Shenando," "Shanidore" and "Tschanator."

The name, according to the noted Rockingham County historian John W. Wayland, was first affixed to the river itself, rather than the valley; please note that Rockingham County, my own ancestral home, is the very source of the North Fork of the Shenandoah River, as it comes out of our mountains through Brock's Gap. Wayland states that the term means "Daughter of the Sky" or "Daughter of the Stars." My own family has local Indian blood; our tradition is that the term means "Daughter of the Moon."

In recent years, many outside of Virginia have attempted to appropriate our name: witness the "Shenandoah Valley" wines of California and John Denver's song "Country Road," in which he locates our river in West Virginia. Now the Iroquois of New York wish to have it. Please, leave Shenandoah to the Virginians.

—*Rick Rio*

'Skenandoah' (Cont'd.)

You might call this "Skenandoah's Pride, Take Three!"

In life there is one great truth: People who argue with each other often each possess *part* of the whole story. This is a good thing for a newspaper to bear in mind! My part of the whole story is this: Skenandoah and Shenandoah do have a direct relation with each other.

Skenandoah was my grandfather's grandmother's father (which makes Mitchell Bush [Free for All, June 21] and me cousins). Skenandoah called my grandfather's grandmother "the tablet on which I write the tellings of my life." One of those "tellings" describes a journey Skenandoah took—probably before the French and Indian War (1750s)—to find his cousins, the Cherokee, and discuss the situation with them. On the way he passed through a broad and beautiful valley.

"What do you call this place?" he asked some local hunters using sign language.

"Shenandoah," they replied out loud. Whereupon he burst into gales of laughter.

"It is very kind of you to make me feel so at home! You have evidently named this valley after me. Some call me Skenandoah."

Native Americans—and certainly the Iroquois peoples—are great at joking. Skenandoah was the "joking name" of an outstanding diplomat, warrior and thinker. I can imagine him going home and telling everyone, "They named the valley after me."

Laughter keeps your head on straight.

Paula Underwoods letter to the
Washington Post, *July 12, 1986* >

The Shenandoah River flows North through the broad Shenandoah Valley west of the Blue Ridge Mountains and into the Potomac River not too far from Harper's Ferry. The North Fork of the Shenandoah joins the main river north of Front Royal. In the Colonial times during which much of these stories take place, the Appalachian Range, of which the Blue Ridge is a part, marked the western edge of the Colonial world.

FRANKLIN - Printer of Indian Treaties

A major activity in Benjamin Franklin's print shop began in 1736 when he started printing accounts of Indian treaty councils with the colonials, continuing this practice until 1762.

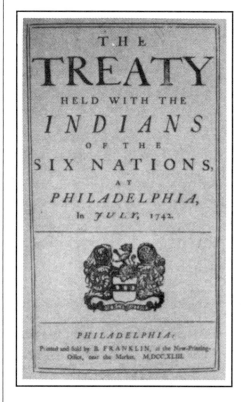

Franklin was appointed by Pennsylvania to be a Commissioner for their Indian affairs and experienced first hand the many formal governmental occasions where the various Iroquois Nations negotiated trade and policy matters on an equal basis with colonial governments. These Councils were highly ceremonial, with much oratory on all sides and exchanging of wampum belts. They were conducted on Indian terms. Franklin became particularly noted for his printing accounts of these Councils.

Franklin was close to Conrad Weiser, Pennsylvania's chief Indian interpreter, sending his son, Billy at age 19 with Weiser to Logstown on the Ohio River to negotiate with the Iroquois. Weiser brought Franklin his account of the Lancaster council of July 4, 1744. Franklin ran 200 extra copies of this important meeting to send to England.

It may be hard for some to understand, in this era when Native Americans are virtually invisible, what an important role they played in this country's evolving democracy.

ADDENDUM III - Chronologies

A. Benjamin Franklin: Some Indian Connections

1705 — Franklin was born and grew up in Boston. He tells of learning to swim as a boy. *Skenandoah's Song* tells of a young Mohawk boy being sent to help young Ben learn to swim. His maternal grandfather, Peter Folger, served as an interpreter for local Indian Nations.

1736 — In his Philadelphia print shop, Franklin begins printing accounts of Indian treaty councils with the colonials, continuing this practice until 1762.

1743 — Franklin begins an extensive correspondence and friendship with Cadwallader Colden, who served in government offices for over 50 years in NY State, was adopted into the Bear Clan of the Mohawk and was frequently a commissioner to the Iroquois under George II. Colden authored the "History of the Five Indian Nations" [the Iroquois] which Franklin read, appraised and took 50 copies to sell in his bookstore.

1744 — Franklin prints Conrad Weiser's (Pennsylvania's chief Indian interpreter) account of the famous July 4, 1744 Council, which included Canassatego's speech commending the Iroquois form of confederacy to the colonies and using the now familiar symbol of the strength of arrows bound together. Franklin ran 200 extra copies of this important meeting to send to England.

1753 — Franklin appointed by Pennsylvania as Commissioner to the Treaty Council at Carlisle in October. Carl Van Doren says this mission was the beginning of Franklin's diplomatic career.

1754 — Franklin appointed as commissioner to the Albany Conference called by the London Board of Trade to formulate a plan of union and to negotiate with the Iroquois, or in Indian terms *"to bury the hatchet and renew the covenant chain."* Hendrick, the Mohawk sachem close to Sir William Johnson, was chief spokesman for the Iroquois and spoke to the assemblage on the Iroquois structure of government at the invitation of Governor James DeLancey. Skenandoah was probably also present.

1754-1763 — The French & Indian War. Indians played an important role on both sides. Franklin as an "expert" in regard to Indians and as a good friend of Indians, particularly the Iroquois, was involved. This Oral Autobiography has Franklin asking Skenandoah to join with George Washington in 1755 to hunt and provide food for his men.

1763-64 — The Paxton Boys uprising. Franklin was very involved at this time of shameful abuse of Indians by unruly white settlers. He was vocal in support of the Indians and particularly spoke out about the massacre of a well-known Indian family.

1776 — Franklin appointed to serve on a committee to draft the Declaration of Independence. Documents tell us a delegation of Iroquois were also in Philadelphia and that they were honored by a parade and by a formal presentation in the Congress. This Oral Autobiography describes Franklin in close consultation with the Iroquois.

1786 — Franklin receives Scotosh, son of the Half-King of the Wyandots, in his home with "punctilious ceremony, apologizing because the whole Council had not been called together."

1788 — Retires from public and dies in 1790.

ADDENDUM III.

B. Highlights of Skenandoah's Life

Since Native Americans were considered citizens of foreign nations rather than citizens of the United States, they were usually "invisible" in U.S. written records. Further, exact dating has never been important in Native thinking, though it has become critical in Western thinking. Nonetheless, the following dates can be inferred from written documentation or are specifically cited.

Such written documentation matches to an impressive extent the essence of the many stories about Skenandoah passed down in my family. It may remain a question for some as to whether the Skenandoah of this Oral Autobiography is the same Oneida statesman whose name is spelled so many ways, whose service to the causes of this country during the Revolutionary War and the French & Indian War was so great, and who lived to such a venerable age. To me, however, it seems very probable they are the same man.

1706 — Skenandoah is born of Oneida parents at Conostoga near where that creek runs into the Susquehanna River downstream from present day Harrisburg. We assume this birth year because Skenandoah's age is usually reported in historical sources as 110. The inscription on his monument shown on p. 8 of this book, however, says he died at *the advanced age of 100 years.*

1750's — According to this Oral Autobiography, Skenandoah is sent as a delegate — whether by his Nation or by the Grand Council of the Confederacy is not known — on two or more occasions to find the Cherokee in the Appalachian mountains and discuss the problems of the French & Indian War.

1754 — Skenandoah was present at the Albany Treaty Conference, called by the London Board of Trade, where Hendrick, a Mohawk Chief, played the most prominent role for the Iroquois and where Benjamin Franklin and Conrad Weiser represented Pennsylvania. It is recorded that, during the celebration following one of a number of Conferences held in Albany, that Skenandoah became "excessively drunk" but resolved the morning after never to indulge in liquor again — a resolution he kept for the rest of his life.

A JOURNAL OF THE REV. SAMUEL KIRKLAND:
1796-1799 - No. 1

SKETCHES OF MY JOURNAL as Missionary to the Oneida Indians from the Corporation of Harvard College and part of the time, from the *Society in Scotland* for propagating Christian Knowledge.

Febry 3d, 1796 Arrived at Oneida accompanied by Mrs. Kirkland. Took lodgings the first night at Skenondon's till they could prepare a house for me.

In the evening a number [of Oneida] came to my quarters, when I made a short address to them: . . . I had now bro't my wife to visit them, as well as to contribute to my comfort & assistance during my visit to them. The *Woman*, who had now become my *wife*, they had long known, having for many years had the care of my family & often performed acts of maternal kindness to them when they had visited my house; & frequently sent some relief to the sick among them.

I also remarked to them that she was the *person* whom my *first wife*, previous to her death, had twice recommended to me, as the only *person* of her female acquaintance to whom she could trust her motherless Children. . . .

After a short pause & consultation with one another, Skenondon replied in a very affectionate manner: Thanked God to see this day, & for The event, which they had long wished might take place, as they had frequently & for many years mentioned to me; as they were fully persuaded, it would contribute greatly to my comfort, & be a means of my visiting them oftener; having a *mother*, with whom I could at any time leave my Children & domestic affairs. Altho' she always appeared to them like a *mother* in her conduct in my family & treatment of my Children. But now, she would feel that from this near relation, more would be expected from her.

He then rose & with tears in his Eyes, took me & my wife by the hand, and thanked God, from his very heart, that he now saw us united in the Marriage relation. He was then followed by many who were present.

4th. Attended a conference with some of their Chiefs, & of the professors. Told them I should not preach till the Lords day, when I wished all might attend; . . . In the meantime I should visit, & receive visits at my own lodging.

AUTHOR'S NOTE: These excerpts from Dr. Kirkland's *Journal* show the close ties and the very real affection and respect between the Missionary and the great Oneida Chief Skenandoah.

SOURCE: Pages 289-90 from Kirkland's *Journal* courtesy of the Hamilton College Library in Clinton, N.Y.

Mid- 1700's — Skenandoah is reported to have visited "often" at Johnson Hall, home of Sir William Johnson, Colonial Statesman and close friend of the Iroquois, and presided over by Johnson's wife, Molly Brandt, who was Mohawk and the sister of Joseph Brandt (Thayendanega), the famous Mohawk leader. Sir William established a council fire of the Six Nations and carried on his Indian diplomacy there.

1755 — This Oral Autobiography says Benjamin Franklin asks Skenandoah to go to western Pennsylvania to help Lt. Col. George Washington by hunting for food for his men during Gen. Edward Braddock's campaign against the French. Washington had been defeated at Fort Necessity just the year before partly because of lack of provisions.

1758 — Skenandoah volunteered to go to Herkimer, NY to warn that settlement of an impending attack by the French & Indian troops. Unfortunately, only a few heeded his advice. Most of the settlers there were massacred and the village was burned.

1764 — Rev. Samuel Kirkland goes to Oneida Castle to serve as Missionary to the Oneida. Skenandoah must have been present at least part of the time after this as Kirkland converts him to Christianity in 1767.

1768 — Skenandoah was present as an influential representative of the Oneida at the Ft. Stanwix Congress arranged by Sir William Johnson and attended by 3,000 Indians.

1776 — The Journal of the Continental Congress records an Iroquois delegation was present. This Oral Autobiography says that Skenandoah was part of that delegation. At the conclusion of their usefulness in Philadelphia, Skenandoah "moved north."

1777 - 1778 — The Oneida offer 250 of their warriors to the colonist cause. They were employed as scouts and messengers under the "conduct of Skenandoah." That winter George Washington and his men suffered from the cold in their quarters at Valley Forge. Supplies of corn delivered there by the Oneida were, in part, responsible for their survival.

1780 — Skenandoah and two others went on a mission to Fort Niagara in that winter. They were taken prisoner by the British and confined there for three months.

1794 — Skenandoah and a delegation attend the Treaty Council at Canandaigua.

1796 — Rev. Samuel Kirkland brings his new wife to Oneida Castle to visit "Skenondon."

1800's — As a renowned elder, Skenandoah receives many visitors at his home. He becomes blind about the time he turns 100.

1810 — Henry R. Schoolcraft writes of his visit to Skenandoah: "His appearance was most venerable and dignified. He was tall, of stalwart frame, erect, bald, and sightless. There were several persons of the party, all of whom were anxious to see him, and some of whom had come from a great distance. To me, he embodied the idea of a Grecian philosopher - grave, dignified and mild. . . . "

1816 — Skenandoah dies March 11, 1816. He was buried by his own wish and by direction of Rev. Kirkland's widow next to her husband. The funeral service was attended by Hamilton College faculty and numerous students. The Kirkland family published a full testimony "to his fidelity in the cause of the colonies during the Revolution."

SOURCES: *History of the Indian Tribes of the U.S.* by Henry R. Schoolcraft. Vol. VI, pp 509 - 518.

Documentary History of Hamilton College, published by the College 1922.

The Life and Times of Samuel Kirkland, 1741-1808: Missionary to the Oneida Indians, American Patriot, and Founder of Hamilton College, by Christine Sternberg Patrick. Dissertation, 1993.

ADDENDUM IV.

Elihu Root, on *Why the Iroquois were on the side of the British instead of the French and why we now speak English in the U.S.*

In an address at Platsburg, N.Y. on July 7, 1909 during the tercentennial celebration of the discovery of Lake Champlain, Elihu Root, American statesman (1845-1937) explains.

"At last, in this month of July [1609] 300 years ago, they [Champlain and his exploration party with Algonquin Indians as support] came upon a war party of the Iroquois. Both parties landed, in the neighborhood of Ticonderoga, and, with the coming of the dawn, joined battle. Protected by the light armor of the period, Champlain advanced to the front in full view of the contending parties, and, as the Iroquois drew their bows upon him, he fired his arquebus. One of his white companions also fired. The Iroquois chief and several of his warriors fell, killed or wounded; and the entire band, amazed and terror-stricken by their first experience with the inexplicable, miraculous, and death-dealing power of fire-arms, fled in dismay. . . . The shot from Champlain's arquebus had determined the part that was to be played in the approaching conflict by the most powerful military force among the Indians of North America. It had made the confederacy of the Iroquois and all its nations and dependencies the implacable enemies of the French and the fast friends of the English for all the long struggle that was to come."

Elihu Root concluded his historical commentary on these colonial times with these words:

"In all this interesting and romantic story may be seen two great proximate causes of the French failure and the English success; two reasons why from Quebec to the Pacific we speak English, follow the course of the common law, and estimate and maintain our rights according to the principles of English freedom.

"One of these was the great inferiority of the Indian allies of the French, and the great superiority of the Indian allies of the English; the effective and enduring organization, the warlike power of the Iroquois, and their fidelity to the "covenant chain" which bound them to our fathers. The other cause lies deeper: It is that peoples, not monarchs, settlers, not soldiers, build empires: that the spirit of absolutism in a royal court is a less vital principle than the spirit of liberty in a nation.

"In these memorial days let there be honor to Champlain and the chivalry of France: honor to the strong free hearts of the common people of England; and honor also to the savage virtues, the courage and loyal friendship of the Long House of the Iroquois."

SOURCE: Miscellaneous Addresses by Elihu Root. Harvard University Press 1917. Courtesy of Hamilton College Library.

ADDENDUM V.

"Nemacolin's Path" or "Braddock's Road"

THIS MAP shows the area of southwestern Pennsylvania where the events talked about in pages 28 - 36 occur. History books give us the western perspective of the French & Indian War. These pages tell the story through the eyes of Skenandoah.

Great Meadows where Col. George Washington suffered his 1754 defeat by the French at Fort Necessity is in the lower right quadrant of the map. The exact route General Braddock, his army, and his young aide de camp, George Washington, followed up to the confluence of the Monongahela river and Turtle Creek, is not known. "Nemacolin's Path," often referred to as Braddock's Road, is quite probable. Whichever route was taken, the terrain was exceedingly difficult, and they never reached Fort Duquesne. Braddock's Field, seen in the upper left quadrant. is the site where the General was ambushed, wounded, and later died, leaving the young Washington in charge of the retreat.

Roads traveled by settlers, tradesmen and soldiers were frequently over those paths already laid out by the Indians. Our own road system in fact often follows these same paths.

SOURCE: *Indian Paths of Pennsylvania* (#71. Nemacolin's Path, Map on p. 111.) by Paul A.W. Wallace, Pennsylvania Historical and Museum Commission, Harrisburg 1993. The map is reproduced here with their permission.

ADDENDUM VI.
THE GREAT TREE OF PEACE:
Symbol of the Iroquois Confederacy

When the Confederation of Five (later Six) Iroquois Nations was established about a thousand years ago, an evergreen tree was selected to represent the constantly living nature of the Confederacy. My father explained that its many needles represented the individuals in each Nation. The bundles of needles represented families. Twigs supporting their gathered bundles represented the clans. United on branches they represented whole nations. The trunk of this Great Tree, represented the Confederacy and symbolized the unity of Earth and Sky as two aspects of Life that nourish us.

Without this Tree, the individual needles would die - - yet without the individual needles, the tree would also die. Evergreens are "always living" not because the needles never die, but because they keep their needles for three years. To the People, this represented the grandparent, parent, and grandchildren generations. The needles formed in previous generations had fallen from the tree, providing sustenance for its roots. The needles of future generations, as yet unformed, were implied in the growth buds. And the Tree lived.

From this Great Tree grew four White Roots of Peace, representing the Four Directions. The Five Nations each buried a war hatchet under these roots, vowing never again to war against each other. The People placed an Eagle at the top of the Tree, as Eagle flies so high that he, that she, can see changes coming a long way off and alert the People in time to consult with one another and decide how to take appropriate action.

All major decisions were made with their impact on the Seventh Generation hence in mind. How would this affect the grandchildren's grandchildren? And after them, the children.

This living evergreen represented the way the Iroquois understood the confederated structure. It was the most highly evolved of the several Native American confederated democracies up and down the Eastern Edge of Turtle Island (the Native American name for the North American continent.) It was the one with which Benjamin Franklin was most familiar and after which he modeled his Albany Plan of Union in 1754. This plan became the basis for the constitution of the colony (later the state) of New York, from which the United States Articles of Confederation were taken. Many elements in the Articles of Confederation were incorporated into our present Constitution, maintaining a continuous line from the Iroquois document to our own.

Three Ways of Looking at the Author

[EDITOR'S NOTE: I have often heard Paula relate how her father would ask her to say back to him in three different ways what she had just learned. He would also ask her to explain her ideas three times in three different ways — once for each ear and once for the heart. Here I speak about Paula in three different ways. ~~ Jeanne Lamar Slobod.]

I. For the Left Ear — A Brief Bio of Paula Underwood

Founder, developer, and Executive Director of The Past Is Prologue Learning Way (PIP) — is the author of many books and articles stemming from the oral tradition of her Iroquois ancestors. These writings hold thousands of years of Gathered Wisdom on which PIP is based. PIP has 57 Certified Trainers (CTs), as of 1996, around the country who are professionals in education, psychotherapy, or corporate consultation, a number which is steadily growing.

Paula's decades of experience in international affairs, economics, and business enhance her ability to apply this Ancient Wisdom to present-day realities. She conducts six weekend retreats each year to enable new learning and holds a number of advisory and consultation positions with international organizations and corporations. Herman Miller, the Lafeber Company, Xerox and Xerox Business Services number among her clients.

II. For the Right Ear — See Paula through the eyes of those who have read her books or taken her training

• "I see this tradition as a circle connecting Past - Present - Future, a sustainable Future founded on Wisdom that has gone before. To me, Paula is someone who carries the Circle in herself, so others can see and remember." . . . *Ipec Kursat, Consultant, on Community in Organizations, New York .*

• "Like a huge, unbroken rhythmic circle dance spanning many seasons and many lives, the oral tradition of Paula Underwood is an invitation to feel the beat. It is a dance of learning to be shared, yet it is a dance that celebrates diversity and encourages individual expression. I marvel at the creativity, energy and sense of community it has inspired in the lives I have seen it touch, including my own." . . . *Dora Ruffner, Director of Wellness, Incarnate Word College, Texas.*

• "I have found that Paula's work opens doors for those who are willing to learn by examining their own stories of pain. Tools such as the Rule of Six have been invaluable to the counseling professionals I train, and the insights of how story and learning walk together have become a bedrock of my new book, The Healing Art of Storytelling." . . . *Richard Stone, Managing Partner, StoryWork Institute, Florida.*

- "A thousand thanks for *The Walking People.* I'm a book lover who has always felt some strange sort of longing toward the Native Americans. For those who are having tough times, your histories show how 'purpose can overcome circumstance.'" . . . *Caroleigh Regan, a Reader in Colorado.*

- "It is a pleasure to watch a true master teacher at work." . . . *Peter Brown, Director, Environmental Education, University of Maryland.*

III. For the Heart: A glimpse of Paula in her own poetic words:

SPIRIT IDENTITY

I am what I am
As all things are.
My right to be what I am
Unquestionable
Though questioned.

Scots and Irish and English
Form a braid of many colors
That I wear with no small pride
Decorating life.

Welsh and Flemish
        and Norwegian
Lend their varying spice
To an otherwise bland diet,
Enhancing life.

French Huguenot
        and Pallatine German
Lend their Spirit insistence
To a quest for understanding,
Perceiving life.

Cherokee and Naraganset
        and Oneida
Lend welcoming arms
To an old land, a new land,
Embracing life.

All these figures dance together,
Their variable patterns
        forming a circle.
Within the center of that circle
I stand.

My Spirit dancing
In the center of that circle
Sings an old song, a new song
Enjoying life.

I watch from the center of
        my spinning circle,
Dancing, dancing all the while,
Marking the path of other circles,
Relishing life.

Bibliography and References

Aldridge, Alfred Owen; *Benjamin Franklin* , Lippencott, 1965.

Barber, John W. and Henry Howe; "Oneida County", in *Historical Collections of the State of New York: Geographical Descriptions of Every Township in the State* , S. Tuttle, New York, 1841; pp. 361-365.

Bush, Mitchell Jr.; "Skenandoah's Pride" Letter to the Editor of *The Washington Post* , 21 June 1986, p. A22.

—, *The Clinton (New York) Courier* , "At the Grave of Skenandoah: Marker Placed by the D.A.R.", 26 June 1912.

Colden, Cadwallader; *The History of the Five Indian Nations* , Reprinted by Cornell University Press, 1958.

Dillon, Richard H.; *North American Indian Wars*; published by Facts of File, NYC; Produced by Bison Books, Greenwich, CT, 1993.

—, *Documentary History of Hamilton College,* published by the College, Clinton, N.Y., 1922. pp. 90 - 94.

Edwards, Mike W.; "Shenandoah, I Long to Hear You", *The National Geographic* , April 1970.

—, *The Founding Fathers, Vol. I — Benjamin Franklin: A Biography in His Own Words* ; Thomas Fleming, Editor, Introduction by Whitfield J. Bell, Jr., Librarian for the American Philosophical Society, Newsweek, NY, 1972.

Grinde, Prof. Donald A. Jr.; *Exemplars of Liberty* , University of California at Los Angeles: American Indian Studies Center, 1991; pp. 144-149.

Johansen, Bruce E.; *Forgotten Founders: Benjamin Franklin, the Iroquois, and the Rationale for the American Revolution* , Gambit Publishers, Ipswich, MA, 1982.

—, *Journals of the Continental Congress 1774-1789, Volume V, 1776* ; June 5 - October 8, Government Printing Office, Washington, DC, 1906; pp. 420-430.

—, *New Hampshire Patriot* , "Funeral of Skenandoh, the Oneida Chief, With a Sketch of His Life", 16 April 1816.

Patrick, Christine Sternberg; *The Life and times of Samuel Kirkland, 1741 - 1808: Missionary to the Oneida Indians, American Patriot, and Founder of Hamilton College.* Dissertation, SUNY at Buffalo, 1993.

Rio, Rick; "Skenandoah (Cont'd.)", Letter to the Editor of *The Washington Post* , 28 June 1986, p. A22.

Ripley, Dorothy; *The Bank of Faith and Works United*, J. H. Cunningham, Philadelphia, 1819; pp. 74-79.

Root, Elihu; *Miscellaneous Addresses* "The Iroquois and the Struggle for America", Harvard University Press, Cambridge, 1917. pp. 3 - 15

Schaff, Gregory; *Wampum Belts & Peace Trees: George Morgan, Native Americans, and Revolutionary Diplomacy* ; Fulcrum Publishing, Golden, CO, 1990.

Schoolcraft, Henry R.; *History of the Indian Tribes of the United States* ,collected and prepared under the Bureau of Indian Affairs at the direction of Congress in 1847, six volumes.

Spencer, Paula (Underwood); "Skenandoah (Cont'd.)", Letter to the Editor of *The Washington Post* , 12 July 1986, p. A19.

Van Doren, Carl; *Benjamin Franklin.* Viking Press, N.Y. 1938.

Wallace, Paul A. W.; *Indian Paths of Pennsylvania* , Pennsylvania Historical and Museum Commission, Harrisburg, PA, 1987, etc. 4th printing 1993; Map of Kuskusky Paths, p. 56; Map of Nemacolin's Path (Braddock's Road) p. 114.

Explanation of Symbols

The symbols shown above and below have been chosen for use in this book, as reading such symbols was something I also learned from my Father.

The two figures connected by a broad line represent to me two different peoples agreeing to communicate with each other in a cooperative way. This reminds me of my European and Native American ancestors.

This specific image was adapted from an actual beaded wampum belt sent by Governor Denny to the Iroquois in 1758, asking for their participation in a peace and alliance council in Philadelphia. (See p. 62, *Wampum Belts* by Tehanetorens. Published by Six Nations Indian Museum, Onchiota, NY 12968.)

This design, which we use to indicate a pause in the story, represents three wampum beads, each different, strung together to create a single design. My ancestors knew that it often takes differing ideas to create a whole concept.

This design, which we use to indicate the end of a section, was created in the beaded wampum style to represent a range of mountains broken by two different passes through those mountains. These two different passes seem to me to echo the theme of "parallel paths" that Iroquois orators often recommended for relations between Colonists and Native Peoples. The "parallel paths" meant that both traditions were honored and accepted, existing side-by-side in brotherhood.